ORIGINS & REDEMPTION

Rev. Francis G. Humphrey, Ph.D.

ORIGINS AND REDEMPTION
Copyright © 2013 by Francis Humphrey, Ph.D.

All rights reserved. Neither this publication nor any part of this publication may be reproduced or transmitted in any form or by any means, electronic or mechanical, including photocopying, recording or any information storage and retrieval system, without permission in writing from the author.

Scripture quotations marked (NIV) are taken from the HOLY BIBLE, NEW INTERNATIONAL VERSION®. NIV®. Copyright© 1973, 1978, 1984 by International Bible Society. Used by permission of Zondervan. All rights reserved. • Scripture quotations marked (ESV) are taken from The Holy Bible, English Standard Version Copyright © 2001 by Crossway Bibles, a division of Good News Publishers.

All images from Answers in Genesis are used by permission and are copyright owned by Answers in Genesis.

ISBN: 978-1-77069-745-4

Word Alive Press
131 Cordite Road, Winnipeg, MB R3W 1S1
www.wordalivepress.ca

Library and Archives Canada Cataloguing in Publication

Humphrey, Francis G. (Francis George), 1948-
   Origins & redemption / Francis G. Humphrey.

ISBN 978-1-77069-745-4

   1. Bible. O.T. Genesis--Criticism, interpretation, etc.
2. Evolution (Biology)--Religious aspects--Christianity.
3. Jesus Christ--Historicity. 4. Redemption--Christianity.
I. Title. II. Title: Origins and redemption.

BS651.H73 2012   231.7'652   C2012-906337-1

Dedication

To my children and to my wife Daria who has been the greatest help and encouragement a husband could ask for.

To the Board and Congregation of the Peoples Church of Montreal for their encouragement and support during my trials with ALS.

To Dr. Amar Djaballah, who suggested and encouraged the writing of this book, and the Faculté de Théologie Evangelique de Montréal [Acadia University].

To Dr. Angela Genge and the ALS clinic of the Montreal Neurological Institute and the Lachine- Dorval CLSC for their exceptional medical and practical care.

To Pastors Russ Fisher of Onward Gospel Church, Verdun and Knut Kolmer of Full Gospel Assembly of Lachine, who, in addition to their own congregational responsibilities, have been of tremendous help to me.

To all those scientists who have labored in the field of creation science, sometimes at great personal and professional sacrifice.

Thank you.

Thanks be to God for His grace and peace through my Lord and Saviour Jesus Christ.

Table of Contents

VII	Foreword
IX	Introduction
1	**1** Faith and Reason
5	**2** Two Histories of Origins
11	**3** Science- General Consideration
15	**4** Science and Origins
81	**5** Introduction to How Old Is Time?
143	**6** Redemption- The Hope Found In Jesus Christ
151	Appendix
161	Endnotes to the Appendix
165	Endnotes to the Main Text of Origins and Redemptions
197	About the Author

Foreword
by Jim Mason BSc, PhD

Origins and Redemption by Dr. Francis Humphrey hits the "sweet spot" for books discussing the creation versus evolution issue. Most books, it seems, are either narrow and deep or broad and shallow. Dr. Humphrey has written a book that is broad and deep – but not too deep. Deep enough that the scientific credibility of the Genesis account of creation as plainly read is clearly established and the implausibility of the evolutionary account is equally clearly established but not so deep as to be inaccessible to the average reader. Like a landscape painting where is it possible to simultaneously see the forest and the trees but without being distracted by the individual leaves.

Dr. Humphrey discusses the creation-evolution issue across a wide range of scientific disciplines and does not shy away from the issues that are difficult for creationists. He discusses not one, but three, mathematically rigorous solutions to the problem of how we can see starlight from galaxies that are millions of light-years distant when the earth is only about 6,000 years old. Each area is well-researched and extensive references enable the reader to pursue additional research in areas of particular interest where additional depth is desired.

After all this, he applies the same analytic rigour to the historicity of the resurrection and, therefore, to our redemption that is found in Jesus Christ, which is the second "book-end" in the title of the book.

His closing section, "A Final Word: God, Stephen Hawking and Me" is a particularly compelling story of that redemption.

This is a "must-have" book for all church libraries and should be required reading for all Senior High Sunday School classes/Youth Groups. It would make an excellent study guide/discussion focus for College and Careers groups and Adult/Small groups.

-Dr Jim Mason has a B.Sc. in Engineering Physics from Queen's University, Kingston, Ontario, Canada, and a Ph.D. in Experimental Nuclear Physics from McMaster University, Hamilton, Ontario, Canada. He had a 37-year engineering and management career in defence electronics developing ASW (anti-submarine warfare) systems and land tactical C4 (computerized command, control, communications) systems. This included the positions of Vice President and Engineering and Chief Technology Officer for one of Canada's leading defence electronics systems integration companies and being a member of that company's Executive Committee.

Introduction
"Origins and Redemption"

The Christian doctrine of redemption is inextricably bound up with and dependent on the creation and fall events described in Genesis 1-3, hence the title "Origins and Redemption.

Unfortunately, many people consider the Genesis account to be fictional or merely symbolic having been nullified by Neo Darwinian science. This conviction is used by many to dismiss the hope they might otherwise have in Christ.

I have sought in this document to show that there is considerable reason to reject the standard atheistic Darwinian view of origins and instead to embrace the Saviour and his Word.

This is not simply an academic exercise. Though I deal with scientific arguments and historical reconstruction, which is also known as natural history, I do so with the aim of trying to persuade the reader that hope in Christ is reasonable.

In July 2005, I was officially diagnosed as having A.L.S. (Lou Gehrig's disease). This is a neuro-muscular disease considered to be 100% fatal. Yet in the midst of this the Lord has given me great peace.

The following work is the result of years of reading both pro and con views regarding the issue of Biblical creation vs. atheistic Darwinism. My academic training is in the humanities and Biblical studies. Nevertheless, on the topic of origins, the basic arguments employed by evolutionists are amenable to examination by anyone so inclined. Since evolution presents a history of the world clearly at variance with the Judeo Christian view, I believe it is essentially a question not of operational science, but of historical reconstruction.

It is my hope that the reader will find this informative and an encouragement to embrace the hope available in Christ and that Christians will find affirmation for their faith.

A Note on Quotations

The reader will note that I quote extensively from scientific articles and on a number of occasions a complete journal abstract will be given. This allows the reader to see first-hand what the individual researchers are saying. Since many of the quotations and arguments introduce vocabulary and concepts which may be unfamiliar to some readers I generally provide a simplified rendition of the argument which is then followed by the more technical quotation. I will sometimes follow up these extensive citations with comments of my own and the reader can judge whether or not my comments are valid.

—Francis Humphrey, Ph.D.

1
FAITH AND REASON

After his suffering, he presented himself to them and gave many convincing proofs that he was alive. (Acts 1:3 NIV)

At this point Festus interrupted Paul's defence. "You are out of your mind, Paul!" he shouted. "Your great learning is driving you insane."
"I am not insane, most excellent Festus," Paul replied. "What I am saying is true and reasonable. The king is familiar with these things, and I can speak freely to him. I am convinced that none of this has escaped his notice, because it was not done in a corner." (Acts 26:24-26 NIV)

But in your hearts revere Christ as Lord. Always be prepared to give an answer to everyone who asks you to give the reason for the hope that you have. (1 Peter 3:15 NIV)

MANY PEOPLE THINK THAT BEING A CHRISTIAN IS SIMPLY A MATTER of irrational, emotional commitment- that there is no compelling evidence to persuade an inquirer to receive Jesus Christ as their Lord and Saviour. Indeed, many Christians balk at the very idea of trying to marshal arguments in favour of the gospel. Is it not the Holy Spirit who will convince people of their need of Christ? It's not really an intellectual but rather a spiritual issue. Therefore, intellectual arguments are of little relevance to one's conversion.

Such thinking, however, is alien to the Biblical witness. The three texts cited above demonstrate that Jesus was not above giving empirical proof that He was raised from the dead. Paul was not reluctant to say to the Roman governor Festus that the gospel message was "true and reasonable" and that the events of Jesus' ministry were a matter of public record ("not done in a corner"). The apostle Peter instructs us to be able to "give the reason" for our hope in Christ to those who ask.

Thus, it is apparent that the Holy Spirit uses sanctified rational argument to convince people to put their trust in Christ. Often people have significant objections to the Christian faith. Many times these objections are directed against misrepresentations of the gospel and in those cases I would agree with their complaints.

There are, however, some intellectual issues that often stand in the way of embracing Christ. A dominant issue in our culture is that of origins. If one takes the Bible seriously, one is compelled to recognize a radical disjuncture between the Scriptural account and the standard "billions of years" evolutionary history of the cosmos. In fact, the two accounts massively contradict each other. Many believe that the dominant evolutionary explanation is the considered result of hard scientific research and that the Biblical narrative is simply a religious fairy tale with no empirical basis - maybe with moral lessons -but nothing more.

I will argue that this perspective can be successfully challenged. Essentially, I will argue that the neo-Darwinian synthesis - particles to people via mutations and natural selection - fails in the areas of inadequate mechanism and in deep time. I will further argue that these two failures actually point in the direction of a recent creation and life forms reproducing "after their kind."

I will also address the issue of palaeontology - the study of the fossil-bearing sedimentary strata and its relation to the great deluge of Noah's day.

Since the purpose of this work is to encourage people to put their trust in Christ, and not just a general theistic commitment, I will deal with the uniqueness of Jesus as particularly demonstrated by His resurrection from the dead. The apostle Paul went so far as to state that if Christ is not risen from the dead, then our faith is futile. Since the Scriptures place so much emphasis on the resurrection of Christ, we will look at the evidence for this event and its implications.

I will begin by giving a brief synopsis of origins as presented in the Bible, followed by a brief synopsis of the evolutionary account.

Two Histories of Origins

A. Origins according to the Bible

PEOPLE HAVE AN INNATE DESIRE TO KNOW WHERE THEY CAME FROM AND where are they going. The Christian has the Bible to give answers to these questions. It tells us that God created the heavens and the earth (including the angelic host) and that he did this over the space of six days (evenings and mornings)[1] understood contextually as 24-hour terrestrial days.[2]

I recognize that some evangelical Old Testament scholars have challenged this view by positing either the framework hypothesis, or more recently, a claim to ascertain authorial intent. I have written an exegetical justification for the traditional position adapted from an article I published in the *Journal of Creation*. This is found in the Appendix.

Genesis further tells us that this creation was perfect, without moral or physical evil. There was no death.

At the head of this creation, God created Adam and Eve. All created life forms (reproducing "after their kind") were subject to them and all food was taken from plant life. There was no carnivory.

Sometime after the creation week,[3] a revolt against God occurred in the heavenly realm among the angelic host led by a mighty being who now became Satan (Hebrew for "Enemy" or "Accuser"[4] [In Zechariah 3:1 the verb and noun share the same root]). Before being consigned

Origins and Redemption

to the "eternal fire" he was allowed to tempt Adam and Eve. Genesis 3 describes how they succumbed to the temptation to "be like God."

As a consequence of rebelling against the Lord of life, they and all their progeny inherit a 'sin nature' and have become subject to death. Indeed, since they had been placed as regents over the creation, their whole kingdom fell with them and death entered the entire world. Paul in his letter to the Romans would later describe the created order as "subject to frustration" and in "bondage to decay."(Romans 8:20, 21)

As God pronounced judgment upon the world, He also gave the promise in Genesis 3:15 that He would send the Seed of the woman who would undo the work of Satan. This promise is expressed as a judgment of doom on the Enemy and probably caught him by surprise since he didn't understand the love of God for humanity. This has often been recognised as the first promise of the Saviour (who would be uniquely virgin born).

The Bible then describes how humanity became extremely violent and rebellious against God. Finally, there was only one man and his family who knew the grace of God - Noah, his wife, their sons Shem, Ham and Japheth, each with his own wife - eight people in all.

Noah was instructed to build an ark, a sea going vessel, consisting of three decks, 300 cubits long, 50 cubits wide and 30 cubits high. That is, it measured about 450 feet long, 75 feet wide and 45 feet high or in Metric, about 135 meters long, 23 meters wide and 14 meters high. These contemporary figures assume what is called the "shorter" cubit of about 18 inches or 45 centimetres. Actually, the cubit was probably the royal cubit. Tim Lovett makes the case for the royal cubit of Nippur (51.85 cm)[5] being close to, or equal to, the cubit used by Noah.

Even using the shorter cubit, the vessel would have had the carrying capacity of 522 standard railway stock cars and was capable of holding 135,000 sheep-sized animals. The actual number of animals was probably in the range of 16,000.[6]

God caused a great deluge to come upon the earth and only Noah and those with him survived the great flood. When they came out of the ark, humanity now had a new beginning, albeit still in a fallen world.

Two Histories of Origins

Noah prophesies that the Redeemer will come from the line of his son Shem.[7]

Sometime later, after humanity had increased in numbers, they rebelled against God by refusing to disperse and fill the earth. Instead, they wanted to make a name for themselves and build a city and tower (Babel) from which they could worship the heavens. God confused their languages and so they spread out from there to populate the world.

This account of origins holds that all of humanity, no matter the colour of our skin or other ethnic characteristics, are descended from Adam and Eve and then Noah and his family and finally, from the dispersed clans of the Tower of Babel.

A feature of the Biblical narrative is that it gives chronological information which, when pieced together, gives a total age from creation to the present, of ca. 6000 years.

I shall stop the Scriptural synopsis at this point.

Many today regard the Biblical account of origins as hopelessly naive and scientifically falsified. Instead, they offer an alternative history that is claimed to be far more accurate and empirically verified.

B. Origins according to Evolution

About 13.5 billion years ago, the hot big bang occurred.[8] This was an incredibly rapid expansion of the space-time continuum. Contrary to popular misconception, this was not an explosion of matter into an already existing three-dimensional space. Rather the very fabric of space itself was stretched out from an infinitesimally small singularity at an extremely rapid rate.

About 12 billion years ago, matter began to come together and stars and galaxies started to form, pulled together by the force of gravity. About 4.5 billion years ago, the solar system was formed, again by gravitationally collapsing particulate matter (the nebular hypothesis). Thus, the earth is said to be ca.4.5 billion years old as are the rest of the planets and the sun (though the latter coalesced before its satellites).

About 4 billion years ago, a self-replicating biochemical entity was formed by random chemical interactions in the primitive ocean. This can be referred to as the first life, the common ancestor. As this first replicator multiplied, errors (mutations) occurred in some of the later entities' copying "instructions." These errors were actually advantageous and increased the survivability of the life form. At some point in this process, about 3.5 billion years ago, a primitive cell was formed and it began to self-replicate. Once again, as these self-replications occurred, some of the subsequent copies contained mutations which improved their ability to survive in their environment. This process continued as ever-increasing amounts of "information" were evolving in the coding instructions of the self-reproducing life forms. Eventually, a vast array of life forms, both asexual and sexual in nature, arose.

In the last few million years there developed a creature which became the ancestor of both humans and apes. It would have looked ape-like in appearance, though it would not be identical to modern apes. Often the human evolutionary sequence is expressed as *Australopithecus, Homo habilis, Homo erectus, Homo sapiens* and finally, *Homo sapiens sapiens*. *Neanderthal* is sometimes seen as an offshoot of this lineage though others place him within the *Homo sapiens* genus.

It is important to note the purely ideological presuppositions that form the foundation of this billions of year's history of the world. As John Woodmorappe states:

> In 1795 before examining the evidence, the deist James Hutton, 'the father of modern geology', proclaimed: 'the past history of our globe *must be explained* by what can be seen to be happening now. ... No powers are to be employed that are not natural to the globe, *no action to be admitted* except those of which we know the principle'[9]

Note the emphasized phrases. He was not 'discovering deep time'; he was assuming it as a direct challenge to 'Mosaic' geology. Thus, statements that Hutton et al were finding out the world could not be as young as the Bible said are completely missing the point. Uniformitarian ideology, not objective science was at work.

In regards to the evolutionary account, right from the beginning differential reproduction was at work, and as more complex life forms developed, death was the great creative force in the evolution of life.

Indeed, since the development of sensory nerves with their attendant brain processing regions, the more complex creatures have experienced pain as a necessary part of existence up until death. One might say that universal pain and death is an intrinsic aspect of evolution.

C. A Brief Contrast of the Two Views of Origins

These two histories are clearly incompatible. The first views creation as a result of God's power and purpose while the second sees the universe and life as an accident, the result of random impersonal forces. Another difference is the issue of time; billions of years versus six thousand.

A crucial difference is that of understanding death, pain and suffering. The Biblical view begins with life. Death is an intruder brought about by God's judgment upon Adam. Nevertheless, death will be banished when Christ ushers in the New Heavens and the New Earth after the final judgment. The evolutionary history says that death is intrinsic to all life and that pain and suffering have always been present - long before any humans evolved.

In terms of the sedimentary strata (which cover the majority of the world's land mass), the evolutionary view sees the fossils found therein as indicating the history of life. The creationist views the sedimentary layers of the earth as primarily the result of a vast cataclysmic resurfacing of the globe in the deluge of Noah's day.

Furthermore, evolution holds that there was a common ancestor to all life forms. As a result, the history of life is like that of a tree, starting with a single seed, and branching out in diverse forms as time progresses. The creationist view is likened to an orchard. God created creatures that would diversify (speciate) but always within limits governed by biological (including genetic, epigenetic and cellular) constraints. Man is unique, above all creatures, created in the image of God, and capable of being redeemed through the atoning work of Christ. We are not "naked apes."

There are those who argue that the scientific evidence overwhelmingly supports evolution and that one must abandon the biblical account or reinterpret it in such a way that it allows the evolutionary history to be true and the biblical account to be a kind of theological reflection, not intended to be used as actual history.

On the other hand, there is the view that the biblical account of creation can not only be scientifically defended, but that it has far more satisfactory explanatory power than the evolutionary account.

I believe any attempt to harmonize the two accounts is intellectually invalid - it simply cannot be sustained. They both cannot be true.

Science - General Consideration

It is important to recognize that for the purposes of this book, I have divided science into two broad categories; operational and historical. I first have to qualify this approach. There has been a development in the philosophy of science which rather convincingly argues that no definite line of demarcation can be made distinguishing science from non-science. Tom Hogan draws some implications from this for creation science (and legal cases involving creation/intelligent design.) [10] Since science is ultimately un-definable, the distinction between operational science and historical science is ill-advised in a rigorous philosophical and judicial context.

Nevertheless, we can make a distinction between investigating present processes which are repeatable and investigating a present physical state of affairs and seeking to determine the history that led up to this present reality. Since in common parlance most people would apply the term 'science', to these investigations, I have decided to retain the 'science' nomenclature for sake of brevity with the caveat that Hogan's philosophical and legal observations are valid.

First, regarding "operational science"; this is the kind of science whereby a hypothesis is tested in a controlled environment and results are observed. If these results confirm the hypothesis, then it can be predicted that it will repeat. Other scientists will do the same experiment to see if they get the same results. Sometimes they are unable to duplicate the results and, as a consequence, the original experiment is said to have been procedurally faulty at some point.

An example from medicine has existential impact for me - as someone with ALS. A research team in Italy prescribed lithium carbonate for ALS patients to see if it would slow down the progress of the disease. Their hypothesis was that, due to biochemical factors, it should have such an effect. They published their results when the 15 month trial was over. One group of patients (the control group) did not receive lithium but continued on with regular treatment. The second group received lithium. At the trial's end they reported that the control group had experienced considerable deterioration and some deaths. The second group showed no significant decline from the beginning of the trial. The hypothesis seemed to be confirmed and they published the results.[11]

Immediately, ALS clinics around the world, including the Montreal Neurological Institute where I am a patient, started clinical trials with lithium carbonate. In no place were the results duplicated and patients were taken off lithium after a considerable period of time. Researchers went back to the original trials and found significant flaws in them. Consequently, the rather promising hypothesis has been disproven.

On the other hand, there are many medical and pharmaceutical trials that do work out. An astounding example of this is the complete eradication of smallpox. In 1796 Edward Jenner discovered that vaccination with cowpox could immunize a person for life from smallpox. This was duplicated and became the normative preventive approach with later refinements. Finally, in 1980 the World Health Organization declared this dread disease to have been eradicated.

Though taken from medical science, the above discussion can easily be paralleled in other branches of science.

Regarding the second kind of research that can be called historical science or historical reconstruction; this refers to reconstructing the past by looking at things and processes in the present and attempting to determine how the current state of affairs came about. In this case, one is not proposing (except in limited cases) an experiment that can be duplicated by other researchers.

To illustrate this, I will give a simple analogy which I shall call "The Great Montreal Snowstorm." I wake up one morning and the ground is covered in snow. I take a ruler and I measure a depth of 50 cm. I patiently wait an hour and I discover another centimetre has fallen. I now know the current rate of snowfall - one centimetre per hour. These two measurements - depth and rate - correspond to operational science since they are present realities which anyone can verify the same morning. I next conclude that the snow has been falling for 51 hours at this rate. This corresponds to historical science. There is a problem, however, with this result. I have eyewitness evidence from myself, my family and my neighbours that the ground was bare just yesterday evening, 12 hours ago. In light of this, I conclude that there must have been an accelerated rate of snowfall that deposited the bulk of the snow during the night. The current rate of 1cm/hr is a residual rate after the major part of the storm has passed.

Though somewhat homespun, it does parallel what follows below and it gives an idea of what is being seen in the rather detailed analysis of radioactive dating.

The scientific example I have chosen is the attempt to date zircon crystals in granodiorite by radioactive phenomena. In these crystals one finds ^{238}U and ^{206}Pb. From numerous laboratory experiments it has been determined that ^{238}U has a half life of 4.468 billion years. By releasing nuclear particles (protons, neutrons) and electrons it transforms itself through a chain of 14 intervening elements until it stops at the final element, stable ^{206}Pb. By measuring the respective amounts of uranium and lead, one can potentially date the crystal.

In addition, in the course of the nuclear transformations involved in this decay chain, eight Alpha particles are given off - "packages" of two protons and two neutrons each. Since an Alpha particle is identical to a helium nucleus, it immediately attracts two electrons from its environment and becomes helium. Helium is the second element (and therefore, second smallest) on the periodic table. As a result, it can escape from the zircon crystal lattice. From laboratory analysis, the rate of helium leakage from zircon crystals has been determined, taking into account the effects of temperature and pressure. In a particular published example, zircon crystals from bore holes near Los Alamos, New Mexico yielded $^{238}U/^{206}Pb$ ages of 1.5 billion years. The same crystals yielded helium retention ages of 6000 years with a 33% error bar.[12] It appears there must have been an accelerated nuclear decay rate at some point in the past - specifically within the last 6000 years. The probability that the physical process of helium egress has remained constant through time is far more likely than the constancy of a highly extrapolated nuclear decay rate – specifically since there is both theoretical[13] and experimental[14] evidence to support potential variability in nuclear transformation rates.

This example of the attempt to determine the age of zircon crystals is, in a sense, paradigmatic. Operational science is involved in the measuring of the elements involved and in determining the rates of nuclear transformation and helium egress. All of this requires sophisticated equipment and scientific acumen. It represents brilliant science that can be, and has been verified by numerous workers in the field.

On the other hand, the attempt to determine the history of the zircon crystal is a different matter. We have to assume the constancy of presently observed rates (and no changes in parent or daughter elements). This turns out to be a much greater issue than normally considered. In effect, we are looking at nuclear and chemical data in the present. We look at two distinct processes and derive two wildly incompatible ages. Since nobody can go back in time to actually observe the formation of the crystal we are on more problematic ground in this endeavour than in the operational aspect.

There is, however, the fact that for the Christian there is a divine revelation (the Bible) that does give us the age of the earth. Clearly the Helium retention rate is compatible with the biblical account, whereas the other derived date is not. Furthermore, if the nuclear decay rate was accelerated at some point since the creation there must have been (a) purpose(s) for that (from the Christian perspective). I believe some have been identified, but that will come later.

SCIENCE AND ORIGINS

A. INFORMATION THEORY

The first issue we will look at is that of information theory. This refers to the discipline of studying and describing the immaterial constituent of the cosmos including biotic forms. Naturalism is the governing assumption of many evolutionists - excluding theistic evolutionists. This assumption holds that all of reality can be reduced to matter and energy. Information theory[15] holds that reality consists of matter+energy+information.

Information can be illustrated by a message. The statement, "Love your neighbour as yourself" can be communicated via numerous media. It could be spoken out loud, it could be written on paper with ink, it could be sent by Morse code, it could be signalled by semaphore, it can be stored on magnetic tape, computer hard disc, etc. It could be communicated by many means, being expressed in any given language.

Albert Einstein noted that information could never be identified with the material substrate upon which it rides:

> We have the habit of combining certain concepts and conceptual relations (propositions) so definitely with certain sense experiences that we do not become conscious of the gulf—logically unbridgeable—which separates the world of sensory experiences from the world of concepts and propositions.[16]

That is, the information remains the same whether spoken or expressed as black markings on a surface, as a series of dots, dashes and spaces, etc. Therefore, information is immaterial since it is not reducible in any way to its material carrier.

Information has various levels. One such level is about purpose. The message cited above clearly has the purpose of being obeyed and thus influencing human behaviour in a certain direction. A machine may be programmed or built so that it will perform a certain function when needed. The highly sophisticated Terra code was developed to enable researchers to study planetary mantle dynamics using Super (Cray) computers. An aircraft is made of thousands of non-flying parts, but because of the specified information-laden plan of assembly, it can indeed be made to soar through the skies.

A further aspect of information is that its source is always mental. In none of the above examples and indeed, simple thought experiments make it clear, was any of the information generated by what carried it. Some would argue that our minds and our brains are the same, therefore, our thoughts are simply products of chemistry. But this is clearly falsified by the very fact that they are arguing for this position. It can't be their chemicals that are putting forth the materialistic worldview. It is "they" who are arguing. Who are "they"? They are human beings with minds - an immaterial entity, a self, possessing rationality and volition. The distinction between the mind and the brain was eloquently and simply expressed by none other than the late Wilder Penfield (1891-1976), perhaps one of the greatest names in neuroscience. He compared the brain to a piano and the mind to a pianist. If the piano is damaged, the pianist is limited in what music he or she may produce.[17]

Information may be viewed as a code. To convey the message, the sender and receiver must have a shared set of symbols, which when organized in a specified manner, are mutually comprehensible.

Furthermore, information is not measured simply by counting constituent substrate elements. An example will make this clear. If I have two copies of the same edition of the morning paper, I do not have double the information. I have double the amount of ink and paper but no more information.

Finally, experience indicates that it is doubtful random changes in the symbol-set of a coded message would ever add to the information content. Rather, such randomized alterations would be either neutral or lead to message degradation.

It is true that pre-programmed changes may occur in DNA sequences and indeed in any coded information which adds information. These are planned, however, and are not random.

There is a counter example in somatic cell hypermutation in B-cells of the immune system. This happens with a type of "iterative algorithm" programmed to change a given part of the cellular DNA. It's not the right sort of information increase for molecules-to-man evolution, but it is an increase in genetic information. (Shaun Doyle, personal communication).

An analogy to the concept of a programmed mutation would be a word processed document (e.g., this one). I have changed vocabulary, sentences, added paragraphs, deleted paragraphs, etc. In none of these cases were the changes random but (hopefully!) intelligently designed. A cat walking across the keyboard would be an example of a 'random' set of changes and its contribution would probably be less than stellar. There is, of course, the obvious difference that the informational changes in the document are 'post-planned' not 'pre-planned.'

A simple example of programmed or pre-planned change would be a thermostatically controlled heating/cooling system. In our house, we simply set the thermostat at the desired temperature and, depending on how hot or cold it is, the system will respond. To someone totally unacquainted with the concept, they would be startled to hear the furnace or air-conditioning suddenly start up without anyone getting up to do anything. The system, in a sense, has acquired new information from its environment and responded accordingly - all according to built-in programming by an intelligent designer.

In effect, on a far more sophisticated level, the two above mentioned examples are analogous to the issue of an "iterative algorithm" prompted change in cellular DNA. An excellent treatment on the topic of mutations and information gain is found in a recent paper by Robert Carter.[18]

The above arguments show that there is an objectively verifiable dimension of existence which is immaterial. Matter and energy are not exhaustive descriptors of the universe. Mind and information are elements of objective reality.

This inexorably leads to the question of whether we see evidence of non-human generated information with purpose. DNA manifests all the characteristics of a designated coded message. A set of four bases which serve as an "alphabet", grouped into three letter "words" which in turn are arranged into "sentences" which serve as "production commands."

The whole universe is subject to an array of physical constants and laws of motion, gravity, electro-magnetism, nuclear forces (strong and weak), chemical kinetics, etc. These laws determine the structure of everything from sub-atomic particles to the movement of galaxies. They are represented by elegant mathematical formulae. A well-known example would be the formula to determine the gravitational force between any two masses: $F=Gm_1m_2/2$ in which G (the gravitational constant) = 6.673×10^{-11} N m² kg⁻² in which N = the force required to accelerate a mass of 1kg 1meter/sec. Interestingly, Newton calculated the gravitational constant before it was empirically measured. Often in physics the mathematics precede the observations. Einstein developed General Relativity, including gravitational time dilation formulae, before they were empirically verified.

It is known that even the slightest alteration of some of these constants or laws would make the physical universe unliveable for us, and indeed the universe as we know it, incapable of existence. A simple question arises: "If the universe is governed by mathematical formulae that it has taken brilliant scientists to discover, then who put those formulae into the universe to enable it to exist?"

Information always comes from a mind. If it takes a Newton or an Einstein to derive the formulae, then surely the mind that created the laws and constants in the first place must be of infinite brilliance, since the laws and constants were put into effect at the origin of the universe. This implies that the mind which decreed the 'laws' for the cosmos also formed it. Thus, belief in the Creator is highly reasonable and I would submit that the materialist position is unreasonable.

B. Problem of Biogenesis

It is a standard principle in biology that life begets life. We know that dirt does not produce flies. Flies produce flies and they like to lay their eggs in rather unsavoury (to us, not to them) environments. Nothing ever witnessed in a lab or in the field has ever shown life arising from non-life. Furthermore, and this is important to know, the scientific community (especially those in the life sciences) recognize this to be the case. Two major academic origin-of-life research communities will be cited which clearly demonstrate this.

Some current research tends to focus on the development of a RNA world as a precursor to our DNA dominated biosphere.[19] In spite of many claims, the chemical difficulties involved have led many origin-of-life researchers to be unconvinced by the purported scenarios. Some have even speculated that the origin of life was on clay found in volcanic vents. Others have suggested that the 'building blocks' of life were seeded by meteoric impact or dust. For all of these suggestions there are serious scientific difficulties which preclude them from being taken as even remotely demonstrated. They never transcend the category of speculation and indeed run into empirical and theoretical obstacles. Even the much publicized Miller-Urey experiment, found in many text books, which saw amino acids formed in a spark chamber with a reducing atmosphere (ammonia), really demonstrated the opposite of the popular conception. The amino acids were racemic instead of left handed which would be fatal for life. Stanley Miller himself later stated that their experiment did not demonstrate how life first developed.

Two recent developments illustrate the difficulty with materialistic explanations for the origin of life. The first is the Origin-of-Life Prize® which is offered through the Gene Emergence Project® of the Origin-of-Life Science Foundation, Inc.® The prize of (U.S.) $1,000,000 is to be given out in twenty annual payments of $50,000 each in order to encourage the winner to keep active in research and not take an early retirement.[20] The Foundation's position is that a non-theistic, purely naturalistic, falsifiable scenario must be demonstrated both theoretically and empirically, to the satisfaction of a designated group of top level researchers in the field. Two of the major figures in this endeavour are

David L. Abel and Jack T. Trevors. In 2006 they published a paper "Self-organization vs. self-ordering events in life-origin models."[21] I reproduce their abstract to show the issues they raise. I have divided the abstract into two paragraphs to make the division of concepts visually more obvious. I have also bolded two phrases and a full sentence to emphasize what are clearly the major points.

> Self-ordering phenomena should not be confused with self-organization. Self-ordering events occur spontaneously according to natural "law" propensities and are purely physicodynamic. Crystallization and the spontaneously forming dissipative structures of Prigogine are examples of self-ordering. Self-ordering phenomena involve no decision nodes, no dynamically-inert configurable switches, no logic gates, no steering toward algorithmic success or "computational halting". Hypercycles, genetic and evolutionary algorithms, neural nets, and cellular automata have not been shown to self-organize spontaneously into nontrivial functions. Laws and fractals are both compression algorithms containing **minimal complexity and information.**
>
> Organization typically contains **large quantities of prescriptive information.** Prescriptive information either instructs or directly produces nontrivial optimized algorithmic function at its destination. Prescription requires choice contingency rather than chance contingency or necessity. Organization requires prescription, and is abstract, conceptual, formal, and algorithmic. Organization utilizes a sign/symbol/token system to represent many configurable switch settings. Physical switch settings allow instantiation of nonphysical selections for function into physicality. Switch settings represent choices at successive decision nodes that integrate circuits and instantiate cooperative management into conceptual physical systems. Switch positions must be freely selectable to function as logic gates. Switches must be set according to rules, not laws. Inanimacy cannot "organize" itself. Inanimacy can only self-order. "Self-organization" is without empirical and prediction-

fulfilling support. **No falsifiable theory of self-organization exists.** "Self-organization" provides no mechanism and offers no detailed verifiable explanatory power. Care should be taken not to use the term "self-organization" erroneously to refer to low-informational, natural-process, self-ordering events, especially when discussing genetic information.

What this abstract demonstrates, and what the terms of the Origin of Life Prize demonstrate, is that there has been nothing remotely resembling a naturalistic origin of life theory which meets the criteria of either theoretical or empirical science. Their distinction between self-order and self-organization is the key issue. One can only conclude that many textbooks, media presentations, etc. which present scenario after scenario of life-origin stories are simply engaging in wishful thinking and outright fantasy. What I find fascinating is that Abel and Trevors have written an abstract that could have been written by a creationist - a position that they themselves would be quick to reject.

The second development is the establishment of the Harvard University Origins of Life Initiative. This involves an extensive multi-disciplinary approach to the issue with substantial funding available for research.

When one stands back and reflects, one is forced to ask, "If it is so obvious that life originated by chance, without reference to God, then why are millions of dollars being spent year after year to find a plausible atheistic explanation?" For a century and a half, leading thinkers in society have confidently promulgated a materialistic view of origins, treating it as so obvious that only a naive, scientifically challenged individual would question it.

In contrast to this blind faith in materialistic biogenesis, the late Sir Karl Popper stated:

> What makes the origin of life and of the genetic code a disturbing riddle is this: the genetic code is without any biological function unless it is translated; that is, unless it leads to the synthesis of the proteins whose structure is laid down by the code. But ... the machinery by which the cell (at

least the non-primitive cell, which is the only one we know) translates the code consists of at least fifty macromolecular components **which are themselves coded in the DNA**. Thus the code cannot be translated except by using certain products of its translation. This constitutes a baffling circle; a really vicious circle, it seems, for any attempt to form a model or theory of the genesis of the genetic code.

Thus we may be faced with the possibility that the origin of life (like the origin of physics) becomes an impenetrable barrier to science, and a residue to all attempts to reduce biology to chemistry and physics.[22][Emphasis in the original]

These comments are just as valid today as they were in 1974. In light of this biochemical co-dependence and the roadblocks of information theory and chemistry,[23] the atheistic materialistic view of the origin of life is seen to be ironically a "religious faith" commitment.

Given this reality, the abiotic origin of life remains an article of faith unsupported by any conclusive evidence - in spite of millions of dollars in support of it. With all due respect to those labouring in this field, it can be posited as a failed research program.

C. The Problem of Genetic Entropy[24]

An examination of random genetic mutations quickly leads one to the conclusion that they cannot be the engine of increasing genomic information leading to more specified complexity. Random mutations are copying errors that are neutral or deleterious.

Sanford elaborates:

The term entropy has several uses. I am using the term entropy as it is most commonly used, i.e., **the universal tendency for things to run down or degrade apart from intelligent intervention.** Genetic entropy specifically means entropy as it applies to the genome. It reflects the inherent tendency for genomes to degenerate over time apart from intelligent intervention. Genetic Entropy is directly related to physical entropy as this term is formally used by engineers and physicists. Mutations are the result of physical entropy being manifested on the molecular level. It is due to random atomic forces and imperfect operation of the "nanomachines" affecting DNA replication and DNA repair. Natural selection itself can be viewed as a type of mechanical apparatus that reduces mutational entropy by filtering out certain mutations. Like all machines, the bio-machinery affecting DNA replication, DNA repair, and selective elimination, all operate at less than 100% efficiency (mechanical inefficiency is a measure of entropy). Therefore, traditional entropy, in its most formal sense, lies at the root of Genetic Entropy.[25]

Indeed, since the discovery that most of the non-protein coding sections of DNA (constituting ca. 97% of DNA) formerly referred to as "junk DNA" (Susumu Ohno coined that expression)[26] has been found to be active,[27] it is difficult to say that a given mutation is 100% neutral. The preferred term is now "near neutral." The reason the non-protein coding sections were held to be of no use was that, since they had no observed function, they must be inherited from our pre-human biological ancestors. With the papers being produced by the ENCODE project this has become less tenable. While it is true that the researchers involved adhere to evolution, it nevertheless remains that their discoveries regarding the functionality of what was previously thought to be ancient genetic detritus, are more congenial to the creationist position than to the neo-Darwinian perspective. Even evolutionist John Mattick has stated:

...the failure to recognise the implications of the non-coding DNA will go down as the biggest mistake in the history of molecular biology.[28]

In his book *Why Evolution is True*[29] Jerry Coyne devotes a chapter to "Remnants: Vestiges, Embryos, and Bad Design" and gives as an example the genetic pseudo gene basis for human and pro-simian inability to manufacture vitamin C. He argues that the gene (referred to as GLO or GULO) in both humans and pro-simians show the same disablement, indicating shared ancestry. In other words, similar inactivating lesions would not be produced independent of each other but would be co-descendants of a common progenitor. However, a 2003 study[30] has shown a genetically 'closer' match between the human GULO region and the guinea pig than between human and ape. Needless to say, this is totally incompatible with any possible evolutionary scenario. The evidence favours that there are mutational "hot spots" in different genomes that are likely to undergo common copying errors, and are completely unconnected with anything to do with common ancestry. An excellent creationist treatment of the pseudo-gene argument is John Woodmorappe's[31] article "Potentially decisive evidence against pseudogene 'shared mistakes.'"

As stated above, the only reasons the implications of non protein coding genes were not recognized was because of an evolutionary world view and consequent blind spot.

It must be remembered that mutations occur in both germ (reproductive) cells and somatic cells (that is why we deteriorate with age). Furthermore, not only nuclear DNA but also mitochondrial DNA is subject to mutations. Finally, it remains that no completely random mutations have been observed which add information to a genome.[32]

A chronological issue arises at this point. If the genome is deteriorating at a noticeable rate then the question arises as to how long could the process have been going on? It would appear (see Williams' comments below) that the process has been going on for thousands of years - not millions.

Calculations vary depending on the average rate per person per generation (both somatic and germ cell mutations). In 1950, H.J. Muller estimated, "the total human mutation rate is judged to be probably not less than one newly arisen mutant gene in 10 germ cells, on the average, and not more than one in 2 germ cells."[33] He then added that:

> If the long-term increase were of more than moderate degree, however, the mutation rate might have exceeded the "critical value", beyond which equilibrium was impossible and extinction of the population was (if the conditions continued) inevitable. For the usual mutation rate of man must be not far

below the level which would have been critical under primitive conditions of reproduction. But in the presence of the low rate of reproduction prevailing among most of the technically advanced peoples, the present mutation rate must be very nearly at or is perhaps even beyond the value which is critical in this situation. Under these circumstances even a moderate increase in mutation rate, such as one of 25%, might be more than could be tolerated indefinitely.[34]

It now appears that the human species is experiencing a mutation rate of 100-300 per person per generation in the germ cells alone.[35] Alex Williams summarizes the situation on genomic entropy: Mutations are not uniquely biological events that provide an engine of natural variation for natural selection to work upon and produce all the variety of life. Mutation is the purely physical result of the all-pervading mechanical damage that accompanies all molecular machinery. As a consequence, all multicellular life on earth is undergoing inexorable genome decay because the deleterious mutation rates are so high, the effects of the individual mutations are so small, there are no compensatory beneficial mutations and natural selection is ineffective in removing the damage.

Germ cells are not immune, as previously thought, but are just as prone to mechanical damage as our body cells. Somewhere between a few thousand and a few million mutations are enough to drive a human lineage to extinction, and this is likely to occur over a time scale of only tens to hundreds of thousands of years. This is far short of the supposed evolutionary time scales. Like rust eating away the steel in a bridge, mutations are eating away our genomes and there is nothing we can do to stop them.

Evolution's engine, when properly understood, becomes evolution's end.[36]

The reason that there has not been a total meltdown of DNA is that there are ingeniously designed repair mechanism enzymes that undo much of the damage and remove the mutational wreckage of the genome.[37] Also note that these repair mechanisms are coded for in the DNA itself.

Furthermore, natural selection is a conservative, not a creative force. Natural selection eliminates weaker members at the morphological, whole organism level, allowing the stronger, fitter organisms to propagate without being compromised by the less fit. Thus, it adds no new information or specified complexity to a population of plants, animals, etc. To claim natural selection is a "creative" force is misleading.

Some will object that bacteria can develop antibiotic resistance, thus demonstrating evolution in action. A close look reveals this not to be the case. First, such resistance may be the result of bacteria which already have a built in resistance to the antibiotic, simply multiplying while the others are eliminated. Second, on occasion, information will be transferred from one bacterium to another - but in this example it is not a case of increasing information but rather of transferring already existing genetic code. Third, sometimes a mutation will cause a bacterium to lose a function and said loss will enable them to resist the antibiotic.[38]

It is maintained by many that gene duplication is the means of developing new information in the genome. As Bergman notes:

> Proponents of the gene-duplication hypothesis of evolution argue that a mutation can cause the duplication of a gene that allows one copy of the gene to mutate and evolve to perform a novel function, while allowing the other copy of the gene to continue to perform the original gene's function. Gene duplication is now widely believed by Darwinists to be the main source of all new genes.[39]

In fact, researchers such as Ohno and W.H. Li claim it is the only way a new gene can arise.[40] Yet in spite of the claims being made for the evolutionary mechanism of gene duplication and the retroactive 'discoveries' of how gene duplication occurred in the human genome, the fact remains that it is invariably a deleterious phenomenon. Eakin and Behringer conclude:

Spontaneous duplication of the mammalian genome occurs in approximately 1% of fertilizations. Although one or more whole genome duplications are believed to have influenced vertebrate evolution, polyploidy of contemporary mammals is generally incompatible with normal development and function of all but a few tissues. Most often, divergence of ploidy from the diploid (2n) norm results in a disease state.[41]

These observations are based on extensive mouse research. They surmise that possibly a single gene duplication might work. Bergman notes:

> Gene duplication does occur. For example, chromosomal recombination can result in the loss of a gene on one chromosome and the gain of an extra copy on the sister chromosome. Gene duplication can involve not only whole genes, but also parts of genes, several genes, parts of a chromosome, or even entire chromosomes.
>
> All of these conditions are well known because they are important causes of disease (including cancer) and can even cause death.[42]

It would appear that gene duplication involves not the possibility of new positive information but rather a scrambling of the genetic code resulting in pathological conditions including fatal ones. An example would be Down's syndrome where chromosome 21 is duplicated.[43] Rather than increasing information this duplication results in a debilitating pathology.

The most reasonable conclusion is that the central axiom of the neo-Darwinian synthesis - that mutation plus natural selection drives evolution - is called into serious doubt.

D. Excursus:
Human Chromosome 2 as a Fusion of Chimpanzee 2a and 2b[44]

It is now commonplace in some schools of evolutionary thinking to assert that since human chromosome 2 has telomeres roughly in the middle of the chromosome as well as at the ends it must represent the fusion of two ancestral chromosomes. The argument is that since the ape family all have 24 pairs of chromosomes and humans have 23 there must have been a fusion of 2 chromosomes in an ancestral pongid[45] which led to the development of the human race. This is due to the purported descent of humans from an early ape-like creature.

Since chromosomes have telomeres on each end, if two chromosomes were to fuse we would expect to find telomere DNA in the middle. Telomeres serve the purpose of providing stability to the chromosome and preventing fusion with other chromosomes. As well, every chromosome has a centromere - a region of the chromosome involved in forming a duplicate chromosome during cell self-replication - so we should as well find two centromeres. One of them must be deactivated since two centromeres would cause malfunctioning of the chromosome. It is claimed this is precisely what is found in human chromosome 2. Not only is there a central telomeric region but also an active centromere and a quiescent one. Furthermore, the DNA sequencing is similar to that in chimpanzee chromosomes 2a and 2b. The case would appear to be strong for the evolutionary position - apart from the unlikelihood of two chromosomes each overriding the anti-fusion function of their respective telomeres.

For those unfamiliar with the DNA letters which stand for chemical bases, A=adenine, C=cytosine, G=guanine and T=thymine. Each one is a distinct molecule. These are the four chemical 'letters' of the DNA alphabet. In RNA the thymine is replaced by U=uracil. All the 'words' consist of three 'letters'.

This evolutionary view is well expressed by Fairbanks:

The DNA sequences in the human chromosome are exactly as expected from this scenario. Telomeres consist of many repeats of the nucleotide sequence TTAGGG, and at the fusion point of the human chromosome, where the two telomeres fused, this sequence is found 'head to head'. The functional centromere in chromosome 2 lines up with the chimpanzee chromosome 2p13 chromosomal centromere. The remains of the redundant centromere from one of the ancestral ape chromosomes can also be found.[46]

The actual evidence presents a different scenario, one more congenial to the creationist perspective. First we note that telomeres consist on the plus side of the double helix DNA of 6 bases TTAGGG. On the reverse complement side the sequence is CCCTAA. A mammalian telomere normally consists of 1667 to 2500 repeats of this six base pair sequence (10,000 to 15000 bp). Furthermore, they are completely repetitive with no intervening genes.

On the human chromosome 2, to the left of the purported fusion site, 35 TTAGGG repeats are present instead of the anticipated 1667 to 2500. Regarding the reverse complement sequences to the right of the fusion, less than 150 CCCTAA are found. This makes it highly unlikely that a fusion of two telomeres, each with 10-15 kb stretches of perfect tandem 6 base repeats were ever there to start with.

Furthermore, genes are found within these repeats - clearly contraindicated by the normal structure of end-chromosome DNA telomeres. This is crucial since no protein coding genes have yet been discovered in actual mammalian telomeres.[47] Tomkins and Bergman cite Fan *et al*:

> In an analysis of a 614 kb area encompassing the postulated chromosome fusion site, Fan *et al.* found evidence of "at least 24 potentially functional genes and 16 pseudogenes." In the 30-kb region directly encompassing the fusion site, which should be definitely devoid of any genes, there exist two actively transcribed genes, each in a flanking position in regard to the fusion site (one on each side).[48]

As noted above and also by Bergman and Tomkins, the ENCODE project has rendered the concept of the pseudogene erroneous since they are seen to be functional, primarily in a regulatory sense.

In addition, there is the issue of interior DNA having TTAGGG and its reverse complement. In fact this sequence of bases is found throughout the chromosome. Data from a BLASTN[49] study leads to the following observation:

> ...the results produced a total of 85 significantly placed hits on all human chromosomes except chromosomes 13, 16, and

17 (1-12, 14, 15, 18-22, X and Y).... Interestingly, human chromosomes 2, 16, 21 and 22 were peppered with the 'fusion site' sequence over the length of their entire euchromatic landscape.[50]

Either chromosome 2 and the others are the result of multiple fusions - an impossible situation - or the six bp sequences serve a yet unknown function (possibly regulatory in nature). It could very well be that all the emphasis on trying to demonstrate the 'degeneration' of the 'fusion site' is a futile exercise. Indeed, it precludes the more realistic project of trying to discover what the function of this base pair sequence is when found in the interior of a chromosome.

Regarding the supposed quiescent centromere, a similar situation arises. Mammalian centromeres are composed of repeated DNA sequences referred to as Alphoid DNA. These sequences vary - including in homologous positions of the same genome. Furthermore, even though all centromeres are composed of Alphoid DNA these sequences (the 'consensus' form is 171 bp) are found throughout a chromosome so they can hardly be considered a definitive sign of an inactive centromere.

After a detailed analysis Bergman and Tomkins conclude:
Alphoid sequences at the putative centromere site are diverse, form three separate sub-groups in alignment analyses, and do not cluster with known functional human centromericalphoid elements.[51]

It is reasonable to conclude that the cryptic centromere is in fact an invalid concept. There never was a centromere in that location.

There is also the issue of chromosome genetic similarity between chimp chromosomes 2a and 2b and human chromosome 2. Before examining the actual evidence from the BLASTN search tool a few preliminary observations can be made. We would expect there to be a significant similarity. Chimpanzees and humans are both mammals with many physiological similarities. We have corresponding skeletal and muscular features, digestive tracts and breathe the same air. God, as a master designer, would use similar nucleotide combinations in His creatures in order to program similar 'constructions'. Human architects and engineers use the same technique when they are designing projects - even if the projects are considerably different from one another.

The actual differences were found in numerous reports prior to the BLASTN study. Bergman and Tomkins report that:

...hybridization and sequence-based research of alphoid/centromere similarity between humans and apes found virtually no apparent evolutionary homology, except for moderate similarity on the X-chromosome centromere. Baldini *et al.* found that the highest sequence similarity between human and great ape is 91%, much lower than the expected similarity for selectively neutral sequences.[52]

Regarding the BLASTN comparison of the 798 bp fusion sequence with the equivalent parts of the chimpanzee the results were markedly different than evolutionary expectations.

...the significantly placed hit count was reduced to 19, only 22% of the amount observed in the human genome. This is a startling find in light of the widespread claims that the human and chimpanzee genomes contain DNA sequence that is supposedly 96-98% similar, a claim perhaps related to the fact that the human genome was used as a scaffold to build the chimpanzee genome.[53]

Tomkins writes:

In an upcoming paper, Tomkins and Bergman (2012) discuss most of the key human-chimp DNA similarity research papers on a case-by-case basis and show that the inclusion of discarded data (when provided) actually suggests a DNA similarity for humans and chimps not greater than 80–87% and quite possibly even less.[54]

The paper referred to is actually two papers: "Is the human genome nearly identical to chimpanzee?" – a reassessment of the literature; and

"Genomic monkey business" – estimates of nearly identical human-chimp DNA similarity re-evaluated using omitted data. [*Journal of Creation*, **26** (1) 2012 pp. 54-60 and pp. 94-99].

In light of the evidence assembled by Bergman and Tomkins, the claim for a fusion event in the distant past is incredibly difficult to maintain. It is hardly the trump card for evolution its proponents claim.

E. Spreading a Beneficial Mutation

A further topic deals with population genetics and is known as "Haldane's dilemma."[55] J.B.S. Haldane, a renowned evolutionary geneticist, wrote "The Cost of Selection" in 1957. He dealt with the issue of how much time (how many generations) it would take to fix a beneficial mutation within a breeding population, particularly one with a generational span of 20-30 years. The conclusion of his mathematical calculations was that there were nowhere near enough generations from the putative common ancestor of chimpanzees and humans (i.e., from 10,000,000 years ago) to the present. This would clearly falsify the standard evolutionary historical narrative.

Though many evolutionists have claimed that the 'dilemma' has been solved - as found in many web articles on the topic - many of their criticisms of the creationist use of the argument are, I believe, wide of the mark. Walter ReMine has developed the creationist position in scientific detail in his book, *The Biotic Message* (St. Paul Science 1997). He has responded to critics in detail on his web site.[56]

In a letter to the *Journal of Creation*[57] ReMine writes:

> The cost of evolution is an important constraint on evolutionary theorizing. In 1957, the evolutionary geneticist, J.B.S. Haldane, proposed the "cost" concept in terms of "elimination of the unfavored individuals", and ever since then the evolutionary literature defines it in those terms. Unfortunately, that traditional cost concept is prone to much confusion and error, and it is embedded in the literature as though in concrete. This obscured Haldane's Dilemma and other evolutionary cost problems from public view. The confusion even allowed

evolutionary geneticists to claim these problems were solved, when they were never solved.

My cost concept eliminates the confusion. That is, the fundamental issue is not the elimination of unfavored individuals, but rather the extra reproduction rate required to increase the favored individuals. The issue is reproduction rate, not elimination. In the simplest tutorial examples, we can mathematically and conceptually translate between the two versions of the cost concept. Compared to the traditional cost concept, my cost concept is easier to understand and more general purpose, and leading evolutionary geneticists, James Crow and Warren Ewens, acknowledge it is correct. Unfortunately, evolutionists refuse to publish these clarifications in their journals. The evolutionists' attempts to forestall these clarifications is a lamentable chapter in the origins debate.

A simple thought experiment suggests major difficulties in fixing, not one, but thousands of favourable information-adding mutations throughout a sexually reproducing population with generational spans measured in decades and with relatively low reproduction rates.

Finally, as already mentioned above, there are no examples of randomly caused information-increasing mutations in the published literature. Even if there were some, they would be so rare as to make the purported evolutionary mechanism somewhat moot.[58]

F. The Limits of Change

According to the biblical creation model, all living creatures reproduce "after their kind."[59] Some have misinterpreted this to mean 'fixity of species.' In many cases the created 'kind' (Heb. *min*) is clearly wider in range than the modern concept of species. Modern taxonomy has a descending order of generality (or increasing order of specificity). Starting with the most general, the categories are kingdom, phylum, class, order, family, genus, and species. The latter term is often used to denote a group of animals which are inter-fertile but cannot breed with those outside their taxonomic rank. It has been recognized that sometimes different species within the same genus or even family may successfully interbreed. Two examples of cross-breeding are the 'zorse' (horse and zebra) and the 'wholphin' (*Pseudorcacrassidens* ['false killer whale'] and bottlenose dolphin).[60]

In these, and many other examples, it has been demonstrated that a currently designated species 'barrier' is, in fact, not inviolate. This implies to the creationist that the 'created kind' of Genesis was a group of animals with richer genetic variability than their more speciated descendants.

Indeed rapid speciation is a prediction of the creationist position. An original 'founder population' contained the genetic potential to produce a variety of offspring. Batten explains this further:

> If two animals or two plants can hybridize (at least enough to produce a truly fertilized egg), then they must belong to (i.e. have descended from) the same original created kind. If the hybridizing species are from different genera in a family, it suggests that the whole family might have come from the one created kind. If the genera are in different families within an order, it suggests that maybe the whole order may have derived from the original created kind.
>
> On the other hand, if two species will not hybridize, it does not necessarily prove that they are not originally from the same kind. We all know of couples who cannot have children, but this does not mean they are separate species![61]

After giving more hybridization examples he adds an interesting summation with implications for Noah's Ark:

> The variations allow for the descendants of the created kinds to adapt to different environments and 'fill the earth', as God commanded. If genera represent the created kinds, then Noah took less than 20,000 land animals on the Ark; far fewer if kinds occasionally gave rise to families. From these kinds came many 'daughter species', which generally each have less information

(and are thus more specialized) than the parent population on the Ark. Properly understood, adaptation by natural selection (which gets rid of information) does not involve the addition of new complex DNA information. Thus, students should not be taught that it demonstrates 'evolution happening,' as if it showed the process by which fish could eventually turn into people.[62]

This has led creationist biologists and scientists in related fields to seek to determine the original 'created kinds' referred to as *Baramins* (from the Hebrew *bara* 'create' and *min* 'kind'). The study is known as 'baraminology' and applies to both plant and animal life. As noted above, John Woodmorappe concluded that the total number of individual animals on the ark was about 16,000.

To repeat, this discussion means that just as there was the potential for significant diversity of descendants in the original *baramins*, so there were limits to the amount of possible variation since selection only eliminates genetic information and never adds it. There is no vast continuum embracing all life forms. As stated above, the creationist analogy of an 'orchard' is a valid metaphor for the descent of all life forms. The neo-Darwinian 'tree of life' does not correspond to observed data.

This is because speciation, by natural or artificial selection, always involves the loss of genetic information - not the gain.

Thus it is reasonable to conclude that mutations plus natural selection provides no mechanism for the multi-faceted biota which we observe in the world - either in the phanerozoic strata or the contemporary era. Furthermore, the naturalistic origin of life, the very start line of the whole evolutionary story, has been promoted as a given and yet, upon examination, has no convincing theoretical or empirical justification in hard science. Finally, as pointed out in the beginning of this section, information theory demonstrates conclusively that there is a category of objective reality which is immaterial in nature - thus undercutting the materialist foundation of so much contemporary thought. Mind really is 'over' matter.

G. The Fall

It is important to consider in brief the doctrine of the Fall. Though not directly related to the topic of scientific issues, it nevertheless has significant explanatory power in understanding the data of existence. Furthermore, it could be argued that Darwin rejected Christianity because of the problem of evil, particularly in the case of the death of his beloved ten year old daughter Anna. In correspondence with Asa Gray, Professor of Natural History, Harvard University, and with whom he maintained a warm friendship and substantial correspondence, Darwin wrote (May 22 1860):

> With respect to the theological view of the question; this is always painful to me.— I am bewildered.— I had no intention to write atheistically. But I own that I cannot see, as plainly as others do, & as I sh^d wish to do, evidence of design & beneficence on all sides of us. There seems to me too much misery in the world. I cannot persuade myself that a beneficent & omnipotent God would have designedly created the Ichneumonidæ with the express intention of their feeding within the living bodies of caterpillars, or that a cat should play with mice. Not believing this, I see no necessity in the belief that the eye was expressly designed. On the other hand I cannot anyhow be contented to view this wonderful universe & especially the nature of man, & to conclude that everything is the result of brute force. I am inclined to look at everything as resulting from designed laws, with the details, whether good or bad, left to the working out of what we may call chance. Not that this notion at all satisfies me. I feel most deeply that the whole subject is too profound for the human intellect. A dog might as well speculate on the mind of Newton.— Let each man hope & believe what he can.[63]

Asa Gray was a devout Presbyterian and a theistic evolutionist. As the Darwin Project points out:

> The longest running and most intimate exchange of letters that Darwin had about the relationship between science and religion was with the Harvard botanist Asa Gray[64].

Their correspondence[65] is considered by the Darwin Project to be a model of civil discourse which should serve as an example for handling controversial issues. Note that the correspondence began five years before the publication of *On the Origin of Species* in 1859.

It is clear that animal suffering outweighs, in Darwin's mind, any case for a beneficent Creator. Furthermore, he specifically rejects the argument from design on the grounds of such suffering. At the same time he is not happy about a world that is the "result of brute force". Instead, he is inclined to see the universe as the product of "designed laws" which inexorably operate and lead to results which are products of chance. He, however, finds this perspective to be unsatisfactory.

He was reticent to share his theological perspectives, though in correspondence with people he knew and respected (such as Asa Gray) he was more at ease to express his thoughts. In a brief note to the sceptic John Fordyce (May 7, 1879) he wrote:

> In my most extreme fluctuations I have never been an atheist in the sense of denying the existence of a God.— I think that generally (& more and more so as I grow older) but not always, that an agnostic would be the most correct description of my state of mind.[66]

It remains true, however, that he was committed to the view that the sedimentary strata represented the history of life from its beginnings eons ago, seeing Charles Lyell as the greatest geologist he ever had the privilege of reading.[67] Since the strata evince death and destruction on a massive scale and since the world we now live in is characterised by pain, suffering and death the case for the popular notion of a kinder, gentler deity seemed pretty weak.

These sentiments are expressed more aggressively and more 'atheistically' by Sir David Attenborough in the *Guardian* (January 27, 2009):

> Telling the magazine that he was asked why he did not give "credit" to God, Attenborough added:
> They always mean beautiful things like hummingbirds. I always reply by saying that I think of a little child in east Africa with

a worm[68] burrowing through his eyeball. The worm cannot live in any other way, except by burrowing through eyeballs. I find that hard to reconcile with the notion of a divine and benevolent creator.[69]

Statements such as these can be multiplied. They are not scientific in nature, but rather theological or moral. The underlying or, indeed overt, assumption is that there is an objective understanding of what is morally expected of "a divine and benevolent creator."

The argument can be phrased as follows:
1. God is all powerful and beneficent.
2. An all powerful and beneficent God would not allow evil to exist.
3. Evil exists.
4. Therefore, either God is
    (a) all powerful but not beneficent, or
    (b) God is beneficent but not all powerful, or
    (c) God does not exist.

The creationist response to this argument notes that proposition 2 carries an implied "at all." The theistic position would add the phrase "except for a purpose and a time." This then leads to the following:
1. God is all powerful and beneficent.
2. An all powerful and beneficent God would not allow evil to exist except for a purpose and a time.
3. Evil exists.
4. Therefore, proposition 1 still stands and is not refuted by proposition 3.

The topics of theology and the reality of evil and suffering come up frequently in the writings of atheistic evolutionary spokespersons to justify their rejection of creation. Thus, it is not out of order to consider the biblical presentation particularly in light of the creation, fall, and redemption paradigm.

H. The Scientific Implications of the Fall

We will now consider the implications of the biblical account of the fall of Adam and the consequent divine curse upon the cosmos. Though this was mentioned when we considered the biblical account of origins it is appropriate to develop some predictions of what we would expect to find in a world that has been subjected to the judgment of God and yet with the hope of restoration. Though there are many passages in the Bible which refer to the curse, we will consider in particular the previously cited passage in the epistle to the Romans:

> *I consider that our present sufferings are not worth comparing with the glory that will be revealed in us. For the creation waits in eager expectation for the children of God to be revealed. For the creation was subjected to frustration, not by its own choice, but by the will of the one who subjected it, in hope that the creation itself will be liberated from its bondage to decay and brought into the freedom and glory of the children of God.*
>
> *We know that the whole creation has been groaning as in the pains of childbirth right up to the present time. Not only so, but we ourselves, who have the firstfruits of the Spirit, groan inwardly as we wait eagerly for our adoption, the redemption of our bodies. For in this hope we were saved. But hope that is seen is no hope at all. Who hopes for what they already have? But if we hope for what we do not yet have, we wait for it patiently.* (Romans 8:18-25 NIV)

We note that not only humanity but also the entire natural order[70] is suffering since it *was subjected to frustration* and is in *bondage to decay* and *is groaning as in the pains of child birth* right up to the present time. The word "frustration" (and the underlying Greek word) denotes an inability to achieve its intended purpose. "Bondage to decay" tells us that we live in a disintegrating world. Furthermore, the analogy of birth pains implies both pain and hope. Finally the verb "subjected" translates a Greek aorist passive, implying that this subjection took place in a moment of time. The context informs us that the effects, however, will last till the day of liberation. The "moment" is the fall of Adam recorded in Genesis 3 and God's consequent judgment on humanity and the created order. The liberation will be at the return of Christ with the resurrection and the establishment, after the final judgment, of the New Heavens and the New Earth. As Revelation 22:3 states: *No longer will there be any curse.*

Let us consider some implications: Because it is the creation of an omnipotent, omniscient and omnipresent God there should be evidence of incredible design. Arguments of dysteleology (bad design) would be found invalid. There are factors involved in multicellular life that make it far more complicated than inanimate objects. Shaun Doyle comments:

> There is a logistics problem that exists for life (especially multicellular life) that doesn't exist for manmade things. Life has to be functional throughout all stages of ontogeny, which means that some things will be in places that seem out of sorts in the final design. However, the organism had to go through stages where such designs were necessary. Moreover, just because something isn't functionally optimized doesn't mean it hasn't been designed. There may be other reasons for a given design. Now the design may work perfectly well for its intended purpose, but the designer may have had other considerations in mind other than function, such as aesthetics.[71]

Therefore, so-called vestigial organs,[72] 'junk' DNA,[73] the backward wired vertebrate eye,[74] the human pharynx,[75] the panda's thumb,[76] etc. will be found not to be 'jury-rigged' (a Stephen Jay Gould expression) but exquisitely designed. The endnotes in the preceding sentence give detailed responses to these claimed 'bad designs.'

An ironic example is Jerry Coyne's statement that evolution predicted the existence of pseudogenes. Ironic for two reasons: (1) it is assuming that because a 'pseudogene' has not been seen to have a protein coding function it must be inherited genetic detritus; (2) it has since been falsified.[77] The quickness with which some evolutionists leap to the dysteleological argument betrays a certain ideological ardour as well as a singular lack of curiosity to pursue the subtleties of design and purpose.[78]

The second observation is that we see evidence of the curse all around us. Nature has been shot through with death and decay. God did not create a parasitic worm to burrow into eyeballs and cause river blindness. Instead, he created the tiny creature for some positive and beneficial purpose. After the Fall, mutational deterioration[79] set in and now it has become host-dependent for part of its life cycle.

Either the biblical creationist view teaches that we live in a fallen world that has been subjected by God to frustration, decay, pain and death or it doesn't. The anti-Christian argument that uses suffering to supposedly refute the gospel is attacking a straw man. The Bible never projects a 'Pollyanna world' in which everything that happens is good. Instead, the biblical position, as expressed in Romans 8:18-25, is the most realistic, sober view of the world in any age or culture. It recognizes design (creation) and death (the fall). It also recognizes the tremendous hope of restoration in Christ (more on that topic in the final section of the book).

A further point about the fall is that even with predation, pain and suffering, the sheer intricacy of the organs involved, the molecular nano-machinery within the cells, the mechanical efficiencies at work are simply staggering. The science of biomimetics is a growing discipline in a number of universities[80] whereby scientists and engineers seek to apply the design features found in nature to provide solutions to contemporary needs. This is particularly active in the engineering, medical and materials-science areas. The very existence of this field is a counter weight to the notions of haphazard, substandard design.

A human counterpart is readily available. No one would question the brilliant design of a state of the art jet fighter or the incredible navigational abilities of a cruise missile. Yet their very purpose is destruction of life and property. Many would say that such weapons should be banned. In the age to come they will be.[81] In a fallen world with sinful human beings that would not be a wise move.

It can be successfully argued that it was the peace movement of the 1920s and particularly the 1930's, with the policy of appeasement and disarmament, that emboldened the Nazis and Fascists in their arms build-up and territorial aggression. Because Hitler thought Britain and France would never fight, he invaded Poland thinking all was going his way. We know the rest of the story - the millions who died, the cities that were levelled, and the sorrow that it brought. People like Churchill were called warmongers because they called for military action in the very beginning of Hitler's aggression. Churchill had no illusions about the evil he saw arising. Many, indeed the majority in the west, tended to treat Churchill's moral clarity with derision until they experienced the horror first hand.

A fallen world with moral and physical evil is the world we live in. It is a world that Jesus described as follows:

> *Jesus answered: "Watch out that no one deceives you. For many will come in my name, claiming, 'I am the Messiah,' and will deceive many. You will hear of wars and rumors of wars, but see to it that you are not alarmed. Such things must happen, but the end is still to come. Nation will rise against nation, and kingdom against kingdom. There will be famines and earthquakes in various places. All these are the beginning of birth pains.* (Matthew 24:4-8)

Thus, much of our life is taken up with counteracting the effects of the fall by means of medicine, agriculture, housing, and technological and scientific innovation.[82] Indeed, it has been successfully argued that modern science owes its origins and inspiration to a Christian worldview.[83] The doctrine of the fall of Adam was a particular motivation for the rise of experimental science in the 16th and 17th centuries. The Cambridge University Press summarizes a recent work by Peter Harrison as follows:

> Peter Harrison provides an account of the religious foundations of scientific knowledge. He shows how the approaches to the study of nature that emerged in the sixteenth and seventeenth centuries were directly informed by theological discussions about the Fall of Man and the extent to which the mind and the senses had been damaged by that primeval event. Scientific methods, he suggests, were originally devised as techniques for ameliorating the cognitive damage wrought by human sin. At its inception, modern science was conceptualized as

a means of recapturing the knowledge of nature that Adam had once possessed. Contrary to a widespread view that sees science emerging in conflict with religion, Harrison argues that theological considerations were of vital importance in the framing of the scientific method.[84]

The fall of Adam and its universal implications are, therefore, crucial to our understanding of origins and redemption.

I. THE FLOOD

According to the Bible, the world was judged by God in the days of Noah. By simply analyzing the numbers in Genesis 5 it becomes clear that the Deluge was approximately 1656 years after the creation ('approximately,' since 1656 represents calculating the combined ages and overlaps in Genesis 5. We don't know the days or months of their births or deaths—however it is interesting to note that by simply taking the numbers at face value, Methuselah died in the year of the Flood. His name may mean when he dies, it is sent." Jewish tradition says he died one week before the Flood commenced). The Flood has enormous scientific implications.[85] By definition it would have resurfaced the globe, laying down vast layers of sedimentary strata. This explains why it would be impossible to locate Eden on a modern map. The fact that Genesis 2:10-14 uses terms that are found post flood simply means that Noah and his descendants used names from the "Old World" to apply to features of the "New World." This is the same phenomenon found in North America where Europeans named rivers and towns after places in their homelands. A Thames River flows through London, England and also through London, Ontario.

Genesis 7:11, 12 tell us:

In the six hundredth year of Noah's life,[86] in the second month, on the seventeenth day of the month, on that day all the fountains of the great deep burst forth, and the windows of the heavens were opened. And rain fell upon the earth forty days and forty nights. (ESV)

Furthermore, Genesis 1:9 implies that before the Flood there was one massive continent since when the "dry land appeared" the waters were "gathered into one place." Since the world's current continental masses are separated from one another, this would imply that the original continent has broken up.

In 1858, French geographer Antonio Snider-Pellegrini proposed that identical fossil plants in North American and European coal deposits could be explained if the two continents had formerly been connected. He suggested that the biblical flood was due to the fragmentation of this continent, which was torn apart to restore the balance of a lopsided Earth.[87]

Intriguingly, he proposed this one year before Darwin published the *Origin*. Since Pellegrini was positing a catastrophic, biblical event which was contrary to the academic *zeitgeist* (already committed to slow and gradual processes over deep time), his proposal was more or less ignored until revived in the twentieth century theory of plate tectonics - but now pictured as occurring over hundreds of millions of years.

Note that according to Genesis 7:11 "all the fountains of the great deep burst forth," indicating a globally cataclysmic event. The expression "great deep" refers to the ocean depths (cf. Genesis 1:2). Something spectacular must have happened if "all the fountains" exploded on one day. Is there any geophysical phenomenon that may be the referent to "fountains of the great deep"? The most probable referent to the "fountains" is the mid ocean mountain range which circles the globe like the seam of a baseball. The total length of this mountain range is 80,000 km (49,700 mi) long.[88] It is usually referred to as the mid ocean ridge due to the V-shaped valley which runs along the centre of the range, dividing it into two parallel mountain chains, and is the conduit for magma which contributes to seafloor spreading.

A mid-ocean ridge or mid-oceanic ridge is an underwater mountain range, formed by plate tectonics. This uplifting of the ocean floor occurs when convection currents rise in the mantle beneath the oceanic crust and create magma where two tectonic plates meet at a divergent boundary.

The mid-ocean ridges of the world are connected and form a single global mid-oceanic ridge system that is part of every ocean, making the mid-oceanic ridge system the longest mountain range in the world, with a total length of about 60,000 km. (New World Encyclopaedia says 80,000 km - see preceding paragraph and endnote. [89])

There are two processes, ridge-push and slab-pull, thought to be responsible for the spreading seen at mid-ocean ridges, and there is some uncertainty as to which is dominant.

Ridge-push occurs when the weight of the ridge pushes the rest of the tectonic plate away from the ridge, often towards a subduction zone.

At the subduction zone, "slab-pull" comes into effect.[89]

A proposed mechanism for the Deluge is catastrophic plate tectonics,[90] which as its name implies, is a form of plate tectonics greatly accelerated. In brief, the theory developed by John Baumgardner, et al, is that the pre-flood sub-oceanic portions of the upper mantle were cooler and thus denser than the mantle regions below them.[91] This presented a geophysical instability with heavier material resting on lighter material. Something occurred which caused the sub-oceanic layer to break up along the line of the mid oceanic ridge. It may have been a heavy bombardment of asteroidal objects. As Michael Oard notes, all the 'terrestrial' bodies of the solar system - including the moons of Jupiter - seem to have been subjected to a single stream of crater producing impacts.[92] This could very well have been the 'trigger' to initiate the break up of the upper mantle.

As a result of this break up, the sub-oceanic plates began to be subducted under the continental plates. Due to the density differential, the heavier plates began to sink into the mantle dragging the continental blocks apart on the surface of the globe. Since the continental basement granite is lighter than the underlying mantle, it remained on the surface of the globe but has experienced lateral movement. Magma erupted all along the ridge system laying down new ocean floor basalt as the pre-flood blocks were plunging into the earth's interior. This caused supersonic jets of steam to blast through the ocean carrying massive amounts of water high up into the atmosphere from where it came crashing down on the earth as torrential global rain.[93]

As well, much pre-flood ocean water may have been dragged down to the lower mantle. At the bottom of the mantle, seismic studies have indicated the presence of liquid water below China. This body of liquid water is reckoned to have a greater volume than the Arctic Ocean and is called the Beijing Anomaly. Michael Wysession of Washington University and graduate student Jerry Lawrence (now of UC, San Diego) analyzed 80,000 shear waves from 600,000 seismograms and concluded that the most likely explanation for the pattern obtained was in fact a massive body of water. They believe that this water has been entrained with the subducting plate over the last several hundred million years. They state that their conclusion is tentative but by process of elimination is the most reasonable.[94]

On the other hand, it would make perfect sense to connect this discovery with the Catastrophic Plate Tectonic model. Again, the discovery is not held to be definite but, as Wysession and Lawrence point out, the probabilities favour it.

Furthermore, if the Flood occurred according to the CPT understanding, then previously cool blocks from below the pre-flood ocean would now be located at the bottom of the mantle. Baumgardner points out that this colder mantle material underlies the perimeter of the Pacific Ocean. Furthermore, in the centre of this ring and also under Africa massive 'blobs' of hot rock have been squeezed up above the cold rock. The density difference is estimated between the hot and cool blocks to be 3-4%. If so (and this seems to be the case), then the temperature difference would be 3000^0 to 4000^0 Kelvin. To have an underlying zone that much cooler than the overlying zone clearly indicates a recent descent (within a few thousand years) as opposed to the normally posited 100 million years. Otherwise, a slow and gradual descent over evolutionary time would give enough time for thermal equilibrium or at least a much smaller temperature difference to be achieved.[95] Much of the data is generated by analyzing seismically measured shear flow.

At the same time, much volcanism would be occurring due to frictionally generated heat as the continental blocks were in movement. Also, accelerated nuclear decay was occurring, possibly even at the initiation of the deluge and as a contributing factor, along with the aforementioned asteroidal bombardment, in the "breaking up of the fountains of the great deep." Such a phenomenon would have produced considerable heat, melting rock and leading to magma ejecta on the surface. It is estimated that 272 x 10^{21}g of volcanics are found in the phanerozoic strata. This represents at least 17% of the continental sedimentary strata. In addition, there is an estimated 92 x 10^{21}g on the continental shelves and ocean floors.[96] The distinction between submarine volcanic and subaerial can be noted. Subaqueous volcanics often exhibit 'pillow' lava at their leading extremities. Sometimes they do not, since 'pillow' lava formations are dependent on "extrusion rates and melt viscosity."[97] Therefore, a confident diagnostic of subaerial volcanics in sedimentary strata due to lack of pillow lava is unjustified. This is a point of considerable significance in interpreting the geological record.

Meanwhile, the sub oceanic blocks were descending at a rapid rate (feet per second) due to the phase changes in the surrounding silicate mantle material, brought about by the frictional heat generated by the rapid descent of the heavier slabs into the mantle and increased stress levels in the contiguous mantle. The mantle consists of hard silicate with a viscosity approaching that of steel. However, laboratory experiments over decades have shown that silicate rock under high heat and stress can weaken a billion fold.[98] This weakening effect would extend a considerable distance from the actual place of descent.[99] Thus, the heavier descending plates would be surrounded by a lubricated interface increasing the rapidity of the descent. The movement of these cooler plates would displace mantle material in front of it. In conveyor belt fashion, the displaced hotter mantle material would rise to become the base of the new ocean floor. Its high temperature would cause the new ocean floor to rise vertically by as much as a few kilometres. Coupled with the "downwelling" of the continents[100] as they had been dragged into their new placement zones, this tectonic motion caused flooding of the land surfaces in conjunction with the global rain.

The super continent would be pulled apart and subjected to enormous tsunami type tidal transgressions until all land surfaces would be under water. The new smaller separate continents would be covered by vast lateral sedimentary deposits stacked on top of one another like layer cakes. As the recycling of the ocean floor came to a halt so would the movement of the continents.

As the cooler blocks descended to the base of the mantle, rapid temperature fluctuations would occur in the liquid outer core. D. Russell Humphreys, Ph.D., a nuclear physicist, said a good test of this model would be to find rapid changes in the earth's magnetic field. This is because the earth's magnetic field is believed to derive from the outer core. Radical temperature changes in that region would cause abnormal motion ('convection upflows' - see below) in the liquid core. These 'upflows' would in turn cause rapid magnetic 'reversals' on the earth's surface. This could only be verified in a single lava flow which would have cooled down over a matter of weeks. Since lava contains particles of magnetite, and since when lava drops below 500°C it begins to crystallize, the magnetite will be oriented to the magnetic pole.

If a now solidified lava flow is examined, the magnetite's orientation tells us where the magnetic pole was when it cooled down. We know that the lava (depending on thickness) cools down over a matter of weeks with the surface layer cooling first and then the next lowest, and so on. Humphreys predicted that if CPT was correct then it would be possible to find a lava flow which showed different orientations during the course of its cooling. Just such fluctuations have been found by Coe, Prévot, Camps et.al.[101] They are among the world's leading volcanologists and have confirmed their findings in the papers cited in the previous note. Humphreys first made his prediction in 1986 at the first International Conference on Creationism. In 1990, at the second ICC, he presented a paper describing the process involved. What follows is his abstract of that paper:

> Recent paleomagnetic data (Coe & Prevot, 1990, pp. 292–298; Humphreys, in press) strongly supports the Genesis Flood. This paper shows specifically how convection upflows of the electrically conductive fluid in the Earth's core would produce such rapid reversals. The analysis shows that (a) the upflows had to have been faster than 3 m/s and larger than 5 km in diameter, and (b) each reversal would decrease the strength of the field slightly. All the evidence indicates that the Earth's magnetic

field has continuously lost energy since its creation, implying that the field is less than 9,000 years old.[102]

These rapid reversals have astounded researchers since the normative understanding of magnetic reversals involves tens of thousands of years - not a few days or weeks.

As the new oceanic basement blocks cooled they would contract and, due to greater density, would begin to sink to their current depth. At the same time, the continents would be rising due to isostatic readjustment. As the continents were stopping their horizontal motion, 'buckling' occurred much as a carpet would if being pushed across a floor and hitting a wall. This buckling would be the formation of mountain chains (orogeny). One characteristic would be the uplift of the newly formed sedimentary layers, often in hairpin type formations – demonstrating that they were still wet and flexible when they were elevated.

This latter feature is found throughout the world and is clearly visible to any observer who looks at any major mountain range. The following illustration shows diagrammatically a cross section of Grand Canyon geology featuring the "monocline" and the Kaibab upwarp. Furthermore, it gives the traditional "dates" for the strata and for the time of the tectonic uplift. It is unreasonable to posit that the Kaibab limestone could be dramatically thrust up tectonically after 180 million years (250 mya minus 70 mya) without shattering and showing signs of massive cracking. The lower Tapeats Sandstone would have been 480 million years old.

It is more reasonable to conclude that the strata were still wet and plastic in nature when the upwarp occurred. The upwarp preceded complete lithification (sediments turning to stone). The evidence fits the deluge paradigm much more readily. The layers are water-borne sediments laid down rapidly by massive currents according to normal hydrological processes operating at abnormally catastrophic rates. The event probably occurred at the end of the Flood or shortly after. The flat surface of the plateau (the top of the Kaibab limestone) would seem to be the result of massive sheet erosion as the waters drained off the newly emerged continental mass.

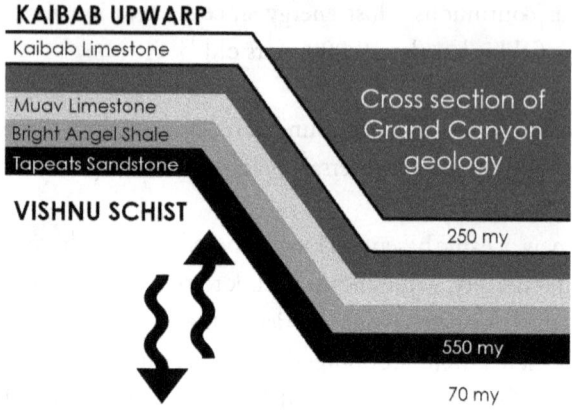

John Morris, Ph.D., PPT "The Young Earth: Science," slide no. 60 ICR n.d.

Tas Walker points out:
Interestingly, the Grand Canyon strata extend over 400 km (250 miles) into the eastern part of Arizona.[1] There, they are at least 1,600 m (one mile) lower in elevation. Supposedly, the uplift of the Grand Canyon area occurred about 70 million years ago—hundreds of millions of years after the sediments were deposited. One would expect that hundreds of millions of years would have been plenty of time for the sediment to cement into hard rock.

Yet, the evidence indicates that the sediments were soft and unconsolidated when they bent. Instead of fracturing like the basement did, the entire layer thinned as it bent. The sand grains show no evidence that the material was brittle and rock-hard, because none of the grains are elongated. Neither has the mineral cementing the grains been broken and recrystallized. Instead, the evidence points to the whole 1,200-m (4,000-ft) thickness of strata being still 'plastic' when it was uplifted. In other words, the millions of years of geologic time are imaginary. This 'plastic' deformation of Grand Canyon strata dramatically demonstrates the reality of the catastrophic global Flood of Noah's day.[103]

Water would be pouring off the continents into the newly deepened ocean basins. This would create vast erosional features including extensive planation surfaces caused by sheet erosion. There would be large river valleys carved out as well. Many modern rivers flow through large valleys. The current rivers are remnants of those post flood torrents which initially formed the valleys. Some river systems and canyons would also form as a result of breaching of post flood ice age dams and as a result of catastrophic melting.

J. The Ark and Post Flood Animal Distribution

At this point we will consider some critical questions regarding the ark of Noah. The dimensions and carrying capacity have already been noted. We will consider a number of questions that often arise.

First, how was Noah able to round up all the animals? Answer: he didn't have to round them up. They came to him. God told Noah:

Two of every kind of bird, of every kind of animal and of every kind of creature that moves along the ground **will come to you** *to be kept alive.* (Genesis 7:20 NIV, emphasis mine)

Second, why did the number of animals amount to only about 16,000 - 20,000 different species? Are there not millions of different kinds of animals? Answer: only land dwelling vertebrates were on the Ark, and land dwelling vertebrates are specifically singled out as unable to survive the deluge:[104]

Everything on dry land that had the **breath of life in its nostrils** *died.* (Genesis 7:22, NIV, emphasis mine)

The expression in **bold** refers to vertebrates since these are the life forms which take in oxygen via nostrils and process it through a lung system and also exhale carbon dioxide. This excludes insects since they absorb oxygen directly through apertures in their bodies without using a nostril and lung system. Marine creatures such as aquatic mammals, though having nostrils and lungs (whales, dolphins, etc.), do not live on "dry land." This greatly reduces the animal *baramins* required to be preserved since a "remnant" of other animal forms could survive the deluge.

Third, what about dinosaurs? According to the Bible, the winged creatures (pteranodons, etc.) would have been created on day 5 of the creation week and the land dwellers (theropods, sauropods, etc.) on day 6. Their remains are not millions of years old (more on that later). They would have gone on the ark. Large animals were probably represented by smaller juveniles. The dinosaurs that came off the Ark multiplied and scattered near and far. People-groups around the world have stories of large reptilian creatures known today by the Greek term *drakon* (dragon).

The Bible speaks of large reptilian creatures being contemporaneous with man. In the Greek translation of the Hebrew Old Testament (the LXX) the Hebrew *taniyn* is rendered by the aforementioned *drakon*. *Taniyn* is also used of large marine creatures - mammal or reptile (Genesis 1:21). Thus, the KJV rendered it "dragon". Modern translations prefer 'jackal' but this may not be as accurate a rendering.

In Job 40:15-24, God describes a creature called "Behemoth." The description corresponds to a large sauropod such as Apatosaurus, Brachiosaurus, etc. Again, in Job 41, God speaks of "Leviathan" whose description is remarkably like that of a sarcosuchus - a ferocious (40 foot long, 8 ton) saltwater crocodile which according to evolutionists became extinct 100,000,000 years ago. As will be shown later, there are serious scientific problems with evolutionary deep time.

Fourth, what about feeding the animals? Wouldn't carnivores eat their fellow passengers? What about monophagic animals that only eat one kind of food? These and many other questions are dealt with in detail by John Woodmorappe's *Noah's Ark: A Feasibility Study*. Here we will consider the two issues of carnivory and monophagic diets. Dried meats, tortoises[105] and compressed grain pellets could have sustained the carnivores. Woodmorappe goes into a considerable, highly documented demonstration that even today carnivores can be maintained on diets of dried meats and grains. As far as monophagic creatures are concerned (vampire bats, king cobras, koalas, pandas, etc.) he demonstrates that they are not as restricted in diet as normally thought. Furthermore, the degree to which they are limited to a specialized diet, may in fact be due to genetic deterioration (mutations) accumulated in the generations since the deluge. The same principle applies to the carnivores as well. A final point is that feeding may not have been as frequent as normal since animals in a dark, warm and confined space often go into a state of torpor with reduced metabolism.

Fifth, how was it possible to build a wooden vessel the size of the ark without it breaking up due to leaking? The claim is often made that in the great days of sailing ships (e.g., Nelson's navy with its 'ships of the line') there was a maximum size beyond which it was impractical to go or the ship would spring so many leaks it would self destruct. The BBC presented a documentary "Noah's Ark: The Real Story" October 26, 2009 which maintained just that, with a CG animation of the 'ark' sinking in the near distance as the narrator watches from his rowboat. The premise of the argument is that shipbuilders' techniques of the 18th and 19th centuries were the same type that Noah would have used. If that premise is correct, then it is true that the ark would be an unlikely vessel. However, we have written records of very large vessels built both by Mediterranean peoples (Greeks, Romans, Ptolemaic Egypt) and the Chinese. Some of these ships approached the dimensions of the ark.[106] How did they do it? They used a labor intensive technique known as mortise and tenon planking. Ken Ham and Tim Lovett describe it as follows:[107]

> Ancient shipbuilders usually began with a shell of planks (strakes) and then built internal framing (ribs) to fit inside. This is the complete reverse of the familiar European method where planking was added to the frame. In shell-first construction, the planks must be attached to each other somehow. Some used overlapping (clinker) planks that were dowelled or nailed, others used rope to sew the planks together. The ancient Greeks used a sophisticated system where the planks were interlocked with thousands of precise mortise and tenon joints. The resulting hull was strong enough to ram another ship, yet light enough to be hauled onto a beach by the crew. If this is what the Greeks could do centuries before Christ, what could Noah do centuries after Tubal-Cain invented forged metal tools?

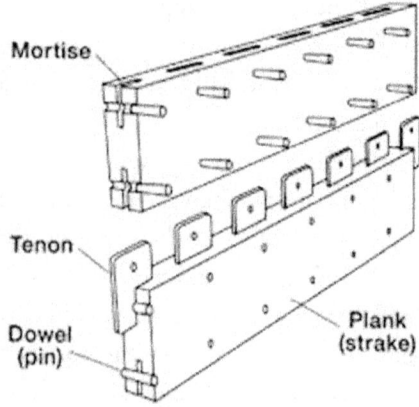

http://www.answersingenesis.org/articles/nab/really-a-flood-and-ark
(point 3 on the numbered diagram of the ark)

This explains how the ark could have been watertight and structurally strong. These techniques allowed the ancient world to build warships carrying complements of, in some cases, more than 7000 (crew and soldiers).[108] Scepticism is unwarranted in this matter and generally based on ignorance of actual ancient practice. Of interest, it is helpful to visualize the size of the ark in comparison with more recent ships. The following illustration does this very well:

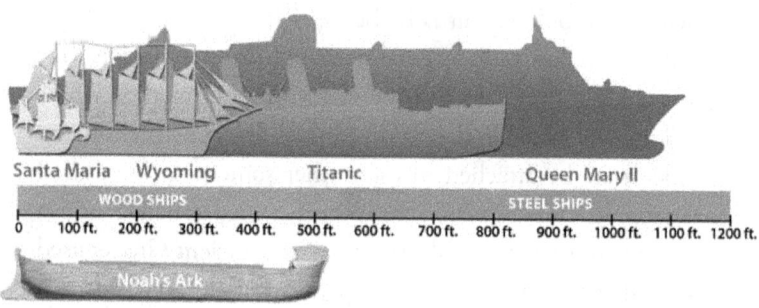

http://www.answersingenesis.org/articles/am/v2/n2/thinking-outside-the-box

Note: the shape with two 'blade' projections, one in the air and the other at the opposite end in the water, as well as curved ends, are based on Tim Lovett's analysis of ancient ships. In combination they would orient the ark to face the wind and the waves at 90⁰ (head on) thus preventing being rolled to the side. A model using this configuration was placed in a bay by Tim Lovett and found to perform very well. A model using the same dimensions, but built as a rectangular box, turned parallel to the waves. It did not capsize, but it would have been a stomach turning experience. This experiment is seen in the AIG DVD entitled "Noah's Ark: Thinking Outside the Box."

Sixth, in spite of the Ark's seaworthiness it would have been destroyed by 'hypercanes' and the inhabitants 'fried' by Accelerated Radiactive Decay of bodily ^{14}C, ^{40}K, etc. This criticism neglects the fact that God's purpose was to protect and preserve Noah and the Ark passengers and so He did.

Seventh, the issue of biogeographic distribution after the flood is presented by Richard Dawkins as a fatal flaw in the biblical account. Professor Jerry Coyne of University of Chicago states:

> The biogeographic evidence for evolution is now so powerful that I have never seen a creationist book, article, or lecture that has tried to refute it. Creationists simply pretend that the evidence doesn't exist.[109]

To claim that creationists never address this issue is not only unwarranted but absolutely astounding. It is generally recognized, by friend and foe alike, that Morris and Whitcomb launched the modern creation science movement in 1961 with their book *The Genesis Flood*.[110] They devote pages 79-86 to the dispersion of animals from Ararat throughout the globe with particular attention to marsupials and edentates. Since this was such a watershed book, one would assume a critic to at least have a passing awareness of its contents. A further example is John Woodmorrappe's 1990 paper "Causes for the Biogeographic Distribution of Land Vertebrates After the Flood," *Proceedings of the 2ⁿᵈ International Conference on Creationism* Vol. 11(1990) pp.361-367. The ICC has been held 1986, 1990, 1994, 1998, 2003 and 2008 and is held at Geneva College in Pennsylvania. The next one will be in 2013. The reason I give these details is simple. Professor Coyne has stated that creationists never address the issue and act like it doesn't exist. Yet here we have a paper presented nineteen years prior to his book and twenty nine years after *The Genesis Flood*. The ICC is a widely publicised gathering of creation scientists whose proceedings are easily available to anyone with a modicum of interest.

Furthermore, Morris and Whitcomb and the Woodmorrappe paper are not alone. The topic has been dealt with numerous times by creation scientists. Andrew Snelling's *Earth's Catastrophic Past*, volume 1, chapters 24 and 25 (pages 163-181) deals with post-flood animal distribution. Topics dealt with are "Australian marsupials, rapid animal dispersion, rapid breeding and diversification."[111] Admittedly, since both Snelling and Coyne published their respective books in 2009 it is unfair to criticize Coyne's lack of awareness of Snelling's work on the topic.

Briefly stated, the solution involves an animal dispersion immediately after the Deluge - unlike humans who only dispersed from Babel several generations later (five if Peleg is named for the event at Babel: see Gen 10:25). It further invokes a post flood ice age which would lower sea levels and open up land bridges enabling enhanced migratory patterns. It would also call for rapid speciation among the "created kinds" due to genetic bottlenecking, founder effects, etc. It also recognizes that slow moving edentates such as the giant sloth are probably genetically compromised from their ancestors - though this mutational deterioration does not interfere with their current habitats. It also allows for some animals to be transported on storm driven vegetation mats. Darwin himself suggested this latter method of transporting land iguanas from South America to the Galapagos Islands after which speciation occurred, forming an aquatic iguana distinct from the strictly terrestrial kind. In this he was stating exactly what a creationist would say. Another method of animal distribution would be human transportation (intentional and nonintentional).

Both Professor Coyne and Professor Dawkins invoke plate tectonics and slow continental separation over millions of years to account for biogeographic distribution. Darwin and early evolutionists, on the contrary, believed in static continents and used that to explain the topic. If evolution is a proposed explanation for two opposite views of earth history, then I would question its explanatory necessity.

Some might argue that since creationists have argued for and against catastrophic plate tectonics[112] they have the same problem. This criticism fails since neither camp of creationists would question that the current continental configuration is post flood - and that is the only configuration that applies to the issue at hand.

It can be successfully argued that the creationist explanation for animal dispersion from Ararat throughout the world fits the evidence far better than the evolutionary one does.

The issue of fossil bearing strata is a significant part of Creationist and Evolutionist paradigms. Though I will deal with the narrower issue of fossil order, I will commence by looking at two 'macro' issues. The first big picture item is the actual statistics of fossil data with evidence of rapid fossil formation. The second is the sheer size of the fossil bearing sedimentary strata indicating a global resurfacing of the planet by vast amounts of moving water.

K. The Nature of the Fossil Record

The following figures are based on Andrew Snelling, Ph.D. "Where are all the human fossils?" *Creation ex Nihilo* Feb 1992 Vol.14 no.1 and K.P. Wise, Ph.D.: "The Flood and the Fossil Record" an informal talk given at the Institute for Creation Research, San Diego, Aug. 17, 1988.

Approx. 100,000,000 fossil plants and animals divided into approx. 250,000 "species" are deposited and recorded in the museums of the world. The fossils in the earth are numbered in the billions.

95.00% - Shallow marine organisms such as corals and shellfish. **4.75%** - All the algae and plant/tree fossils including the vegetation that now makes up the trillions of tonnes of coal, and all the other invertebrate fossils including the insects. **0.25%** - are vertebrates (fish, amphibians, reptiles, birds, mammals). **Of this 0.25% only 1% of that (or 0.0025%)** is vertebrate fossils that consist of more than a single bone. For example, only one stegosaurus skull has been found, and many of the horse species are represented by only one specimen of tooth.

This immediately informs us that the fossil bearing strata (the phanerozoic column) were laid down as water born sediments - hence sedimentary strata. Secondly, the water source was marine transgression of land surfaces and not local fresh water phenomena. This is not really open to challenge though sometimes some will claim that sandstone formations are fossilized deserts. There is no mechanism to explain the subaerial lithification of desert terrain complete with fossilized animal footprints. Clearly we are dealing with subaqueous, not subaerial formations.

Finally, it is evident that fossils formed quickly since, contrary to Darwin's expectations, we have found many soft bodied creatures (jellyfish[113], octopuses[114] etc.). Obviously, they would have disintegrated before permineralization if the latter took any great length of time. In fact, dead jelly fish and octopuses will be utterly destroyed and disappear due to scavengers and bacterial action. Garry Graham notes the evolutionist attempt to explain the exquisite preservation of the five octopus fossils found in Lebanon and supposedly 95 million years old:[115]

Lead author of the report "New Octopods," Dr. Dirk Fuchs of the Freie University, Berlin, said, "The luck was that the corpse landed untouched on the sea floor. The sea floor was free of oxygen and therefore free of scavengers." But lack of oxygen is no preservative - experiments with fish carcasses show that even in the absence of oxygen they still disintegrate on the ocean bottom.[116] Other scientists have published research showing that the ocean floor is actually teeming with bacterial life.[117] So these scientists have not explained the remarkably preserved fossils at all.

As far as the jellyfish are concerned, they are supposedly 500 million years old (Cambrian Era). Their formation and preservation are clearly the result of rapid burial in water born sediments.

The very phenomena of fossilization bespeaks rapid aqueous deposition in mineral laden waters, replete with cementing agents much like contemporary natural mineral springs where tourists can throw in old hats, gloves, scarves, etc. and retrieve them a few days later as mineralised 'fossils.' Indeed, a leading dinosaur specialist[118] comments regarding animal bones:

> The amount of time that it takes for a bone to become completely permineralized is highly variable. If the groundwater is heavily laden with minerals in solution, the process can happen rapidly.

Modern bones that fall into mineral springs can become permineralized within a matter of weeks.

A second 'macro' issue with the fossil bearing sedimentary strata is their sheer magnitude both horizontally and in depth. Baumgardner states:[119]

> That the catastrophe was global in extent is clear from the extreme horizontal extent and continuity of the continental sedimentary deposits. That there was a single large catastrophe and not many smaller ones with long gaps in between is implied by the lack of erosional channels, soil horizons, and dissolution structures at the interfaces between successive strata.
>
> ....The scale of the water catastrophe implied by such formations boggles the mind. Yet numerical calculation demonstrates that when significant areas of the continental surface are flooded, strong water currents with velocities of tens of meters per second spontaneously arise.[120] Such currents are analogous to planetary waves in the atmosphere and are driven by the earth's rotation.
>
> ...This sort of dramatic global-scale catastrophism documented in the Paleozoic, Mesozoic, and much of the Cenozoic sediments implies a distinctively different interpretation of the associated fossil record. Instead of representing an evolutionary sequence, the record reveals a successive destruction of ecological habitat in a global tectonic and hydrologic catastrophe. This understanding readily explains why Darwinian intermediate types are systematically absent from the geological record— the fossil record documents a brief and intense global destruction of life and not a long evolutionary history! The types of plants and animals preserved as fossils were the forms of life that existed on the earth prior to the catastrophe. The long span of time and the intermediate forms of life that the evolutionist imagines in his mind are simply illusions. And the strong observational evidence for this catastrophe absolutely demands a radically revised timescale relative to that assumed by evolutionists.

As stated, the extensive surface area covered by many of the strata (sometimes continental in scope) clearly speaks, not of slow and gradual, but global catastrophic phenomena. A few examples will suffice. The Coconino Sandstone exposed in the Grand Canyon walls "...contains enormous, southward dipping, cross beds which provide evidence of sand accumulation under deep, fast moving water."[121] The area covered by this formation exceeds 100,000 square miles (256,000 square kilometres) and its thickness varies from 30 feet to 1000 feet. Conservative estimates place its volume at 10,000 cubic miles (41,000 cubic kilometres).

> This layer also contains physical features called cross beds. While the overall layer of sandstone is horizontal, these cross beds are clearly visible as sloped beds ....These beds are remnants of the sand waves produced by the water currents that deposited the sand (like sand dunes, but underwater).... So it can be demonstrated that water, flowing at 3–5 miles per hour (4.8–8 km/h), deposited the Coconino Sandstone as massive sheets of sand, with sand waves up to 60 feet (18 m) high. At this rate, the whole Coconino Sandstone layer (all 10,000 cubic miles of sand) would have been deposited in just a few days![122]

Other strata of the Grand Canyon are likewise widespread.[123]

Another Grand Canyon formation of even larger size is connected with the Tapeats sandstone:

> When we map out the occurrences of the Tapeats Sandstone it covers much of North America. It's the lowest level of what's called the Sauk sequence of rocks. The series of rocks that is hemispherical in extent. This rock unit is understood as being a series of underwater mudflows at ninety miles an hour. Certainly this is evidence of a great flood such as the Flood described in Scripture.[124]

The evolutionary description sees this sequence as a result of marine transgression into the North American Craton during the "Late

Precambrian to mid-Ordovician; about 650 to 460 million years ago."[125] Furthermore:[126]

> "...the Sauk sequence was the earliest of the six cratonic sequences that have occurred during the Phanerozoic (followed by the Tippecanoe, Kaskaskia, Absaroka, Zuñi, and Tejas). It dates from the late Proterozoic through the early Ordovician, though the marine transgression did not begin in earnest until the middle Cambrian.[127]
>
> At its peak, most of North America was covered by the shallow Sauk Sea, save for parts of the Canadian Shield and the islands of the Transcontinental Arch.[128] The stratigraphy of the Sauk sequence indicates shallow-water deposition, primarily consisting of well-sorted sandstones and clastic carbonates.

It is held to represent the result of increased mid oceanic ridge activity in turn causing the sea floor to be hotter and thus causing vertical movement which caused marine transgression of the continent. This process would be repeated through subsequent geological time producing the five following sequences mentioned above. This is more or less what CPT proposes, though the time scales are orders of magnitude apart.

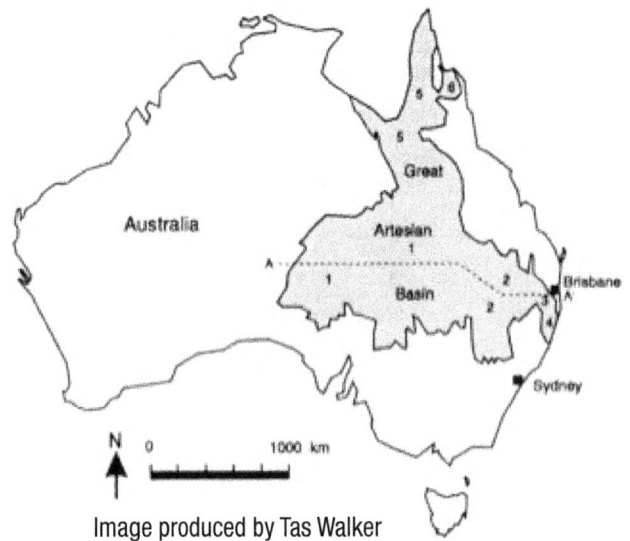

Image produced by Tas Walker

Formations of similar and greater magnitude are found all over the world. An example from Australia is illustrative of this phenomenon, namely the Great Artesian Basin which underlies approximately 20% of the island continent. Much larger than the Coconino Sandstone formation, though smaller than the Sauk sequence, it occupies about 670,000 square miles (1,735,000 square kilometres).[129] It mainly underlies Queensland, with some segments underlying Northern Territory, New South Wales and South Australia. It has an estimated volume of 2,500,000 cubic kilometres.[130] Though evolutionists see this as a 'Mesozoic' formation (65-284 million years ago), Tas Walker has identified it as a megasequence (conformable strata bounded by unconformities) formed as the Flood waters were reaching their peak (the zenithic stage in his geological model). By examining his article referred to in the preceding note, one can see not only a creationist scientific approach but also its explanatory power which I believe is far more convincing than the evolutionary, long ages perspective.

The famed "White Cliffs of Dover" are simply a visible portion of a chalk formation which spreads westward through England to Ireland and eastward across France, Netherlands, Germany, southern Scandinavia, Poland, parts of eastern Europe, Turkey, Israel, Egypt, and eventually as far as Kazakhstan.[131]

> Remarkably, the same chalk beds with the same fossils and the same distinctive strata above and below them are also found in the Midwest USA, from Nebraska in the north to Texas in the south. They also appear in the Perth Basin of Western Australia.[132]

Furthermore, as Baumgardner points out, the layers were laid down without substantial intervening time periods.

Regarding fossil order, it is important to consider the preceding information. The sheer magnitude of these sedimentary formations, the inductively derived depths and velocities of the water currents involved, and the fact that the layers appear to be laid down in rapid succession would indicate (as Baumgardner notes) that they are the product of a single global cataclysmic event. By definition, all the buried biota would have been living at the same time.

There would be a tendency for similar creatures and plants to be found in similar sedimentary strata, that is, there would be a natural sorting of remains. The reasons would include ecological zonation - what Baumgardner calls "a successive destruction of ecological habitat in a global tectonic and hydrologic catastrophe."[133]

Another tendency would be the phenomenon of hydrological sorting wherein objects in a flowing current are deposited in separate strata due their different shapes and masses.

In fact, sediment experiments[134] have shown that as a current advances, the minerals carried therein are deposited in strata in such a way that a particle situated on the bottom strata would be laid down by the advancing current *after* particles deposited in higher strata back of the depositional front. The current is depositing particles which self separate according to their respective physical properties. As the current moves, it lays down material at the bottom first, but the second stratum of particles has been deposited before those at the forefront of the advancing bottom strata. This means that a particle "A" was laid down in the second strata at horizontal distance (from start) D and particle "B" was deposited in the advancing bottom strata at D+E (E=horizontal distance between deposition of "A" and "B"). Thus particle "B" though in a lower stratum than "A" was actually laid down after "A".

This has enormous implications. Just as the particles self sorted in the current, so biota caught in the raging waters, indicated by the geophysical data, would themselves have a tendency to be self sorted. Just as the particles were contemporary, so were the life forms represented in the fossil bearing strata. Furthermore, fossils in lower layers may have been laid down after fossils in the upper layers. These observations are just that: observations of flume experiments using flowing water and granular mixes.

Another rather obvious point has to be made. The flood waters would not have covered the continents all at once. There would have been massive marine transgressions followed by retreat followed by transgression in cyclic fashion. This would allow animals to lay down footprints or give birth or lay down eggs on exposed ground before it was covered by returning waters. Normal animal behaviour is flight from approaching fire or flood waters. When the water would be in a retreat cycle they would venture back to their previous locale, only to be either overwhelmed by the next incursion - or escape to higher ground and repeat the process again.

A particular example is the Jindong Formation, South Korea described by M.G. Lockley in a major work published by Cambridge University Press.[135] The following creationist analysis is given by Michael Oard:

> In this formation, over 100 dinosaur trackways have been discovered on numerous different thin bedding planes in a strata sequence 100 to 200 m thick. Dinosaur track expert Martin Lockley explains the occurrence of dinosaur tracks as representing '...groups or herds of subadults and adults passing through the region on purposeful local or long-distance migrations (that is, not milling around or browsing locally).' Can the Flood explain such a vertical sequence of tracks?
>
> Actually, it is not too difficult.... the Flood involved oscillating sea levels. In some places, this would have forced dinosaurs to move back and forth on the exposed land. A thin layer of sediment would have been laid during each rise, and the dinosaurs would have walked back over the same area during each fall of sea level. In the case of the Formation, one could expect that the exposed land would have been quite small, so that the dinosaurs would have walked over the same area, i.e. containing previously-made tracks. A similar sequence is suggested for multiple egg horizons, which occur on far fewer horizons than tracks in a local area.[136]

The transgressions would become greater and greater in scope accompanied by forty days of torrential downpour. As the continents moved apart, temporarily downwelling, as the seabed rose (see above), the amount of geological "work" accomplished would be enormous. As stated above, massive sedimentary strata would be laid down entombing billions of plants and animals. The most abundant creatures would, of necessity, be marine in nature. Since the waters were mineral rich

SCIENCE AND ORIGINS

(including abundant silicates and calcium carbonate) the sediments would harden after the deluge and turn to stone fairly rapidly (years, centuries, but not millions of years).

There is a popular misconception that fossils demonstrate the truth of evolution. Many researchers will admit that this is not quite the case, however. I must be careful with this statement. Leading palaeontologists can be quoted who point out that there are no clear-cut definite ancestral linkages observable in the strata. To be fair to them, they are not claiming the non-existence of evolutionary lineages. They are simply claiming that there are often a variety of lineages that could be derived from the evidence but there cannot be certainty attached to any of them. This would seem to be the thrust of Dr. Colin Patterson's response[137] to evolutionist Lionel Theuneussin's question regarding his correspondence with Luther Sunderland. It is appropriate to consider the original quote which caused Lionel Theuneussin to pursue the matter. The quote is taken from Sunderland's book and starts with Sunderland setting the context.

Before interviewing Dr. Patterson, the author [Sunderland] read his book, Evolution, which he had written for the British Museum of Natural History. In it he had solicited comments from readers about the book's contents. One reader wrote a letter to Dr. Patterson asking why he did not put a single photograph of a transitional fossil in his book. On April 10, 1979, he replied to the author in a most candid letter as follows:

'... I fully agree with your comments on the lack of direct illustration of evolutionary transitions in my book. If I knew of any, fossil or living, I would certainly have included them. You suggest that an artist should be used to visualise such transformations, but where would he get the information from? I could not, honestly, provide it, and if I were to leave it to artistic licence, would that not mislead the reader?

'I wrote the text of my book [Evolution] four years ago. If I were to write it now, I think the book would be rather different. Gradualism is a concept I believe in, not just because of Darwin's authority, but because my understanding of genetics seems to demand it. Yet Gould and the American Museum people are hard to contradict when they say there are no transitional fossils. As a palaeontologist myself, I am much occupied with the philosophical problems of identifying ancestral forms in the fossil record. You say that I should at least "show a photo of the fossil from which each type of organism was derived."? I will lay it on the line—there is not one such fossil for which one could make a watertight argument. The reason is that statements about ancestry and descent are not applicable in the fossil record. Is Archaeopteryx the ancestor of all birds? Perhaps yes, perhaps no, there is no way of answering the question. It is easy enough to make up stories of how one form gave rise to another, and to find reasons why the stages should be favoured by natural selection. But such stories are not part of science, for there is no way of putting them to the test. So, much as I should like to oblige you by jumping to the defence of gradualism, and fleshing out the transitions between the major types of animals and plants, I find myself a bit short of the intellectual justification necessary for the job ...'[138]

This quote has been widely circulated by creationists and for good reason, considering the reputation of the late Dr. Patterson. Needless to say, some evolutionists have cried foul and have engaged in damage control. Such is the case with Theuneussin. A creationist rebuttal to Theuneussin's and Dr. Patterson's response to the use of this quote is given by Gary Bates.[139] The fact remains that, though Dr. Patterson saw many candidates for intermediate forms, he found it impossible to be convinced about any specific line of descent. Dr. Patterson was a consistent "cladist" which means fossils can be grouped into a "clad" due to morphological similarities. Such a "clad," however, is therefore a descriptive tool which cannot give any definitive line of descent. It is this fact that is absent from the popular consciousness. Most people are under the impression that fossils are the 'proof' of evolution because they show an empirically valid line of development. Yet even Darwin himself wrote:

Why is not every geological formation and every stratum full of such intermediate links? Geology assuredly does not reveal any such finely graduated organic chain; and this is the most obvious and serious objection which can be urged against the theory.[140]

Darwin devoted much thought to the fossil record and this is the conclusion he came to. He speculated that the problem may have been due to the imperfection of the fossil record and that further discoveries would fill in the gaps. **Today, the same state of affairs exists**. The late Stephen J. Gould of Harvard University stated:

> The absence of fossil evidence for intermediary stages between major transitions in organic design, indeed our inability, even in our imagination, to construct functional intermediates in many cases, has been a persistent and nagging problem for gradualistic accounts of evolution.[141]

Gould protested that creationists used quotes like this to imply he was an ally. This charge is unwarranted since he was, and is always claimed to be, an evolutionist by creationists. Quotes from evolutionists, stating that there is no clear cut 'vector' of evolutionary ascent, leads to an inexorable question: if the fossil data is so ambiguous, is it not really a question of philosophical presuppositions governing the order they are arranged in?

L. Excursus: Tiktaalik[142] – A Test Case for a Transitional Form

Every so often a so-called transitional fossil is identified and is announced to the world press as a major discovery vindicating the evolutionary story. Subsequent studies reveal it to be no such thing. The refutation, however, seldom gathers much attention and the original interpretation remains in the popular mind.

An example of this phenomenon is Tiktaalik as a supposed transitional form between fish and tetrapod. Jerry Coyne sees this as a classic example of successful evolutionary prediction:

> If there were lobe–finned fishes but no terrestrial vertebrates 390 million years ago, and clearly terrestrial vertebrates

360 million years ago, where would you expect to find the transitional forms? Somewhere in between. Following this logic, [University of Chicago colleague Neil] Shubin predicted that if transitional forms existed, their fossils would be found in strata around 375 million years old. Moreover, the rocks would have to be from fresh water rather than marine sediments, because late lobe-finned fish and early amphibians both lived in fresh water.

Searching his college geology textbook for a map of exposed freshwater sediments of the right age, Shubin and his colleagues zeroed in on a paleontologically unexplored region of the Canadian Arctic: Ellesmere Island.[143]

He then describes how after five years of "fruitless and expensive searching" he found his transitional form among a group of fossils stacked on top of one another in sedimentary rock apparently laid down by an ancient stream. He describes its features as both fish-like and amphibian-like. The latter include a neck (which fish lack), a flattened head with eyes and nostrils on top and not on the sides. It also had sturdy ribs which would enable it to pump more air into its lungs (it could breath both ways - gills and nostrils). It also had fewer and sturdier bones in its lobe fins which enabled it to manoeuvre in shallow water and to keep its head above water to survey the scene. Clearly this was the ancestor of land vertebrates and, therefore, our ancestor. Coyne concludes:

> Tiktaalik shows that our ancestors were flat-headed predatory fish who lurked in the shallow waters of streams. It is a fossil that marvellously connects fish with amphibians. And equally marvellous is that the discovery was not only anticipated, but predicted to occur in rocks of a certain age and in a certain place.
>
> .....The best way to experience the drama of evolution is to see the fossils for yourself, or better yet, handle them. My students had this chance when Neil brought a cast of Tiktaalik to class, passed it around, and showed how it filled the bill of

a true transitional form. This was, to them, the most tangible evidence that evolution was true. How often do you get to put your hands on a piece of evolutionary history, much less one that might have been your distant ancestor?[144]

Richard Dawkins concurs and states in his book, *The Greatest Show on Earth*:[145]

"Tiktaalik is the perfect missing link—perfect, because it almost exactly splits the difference between fish and amphibian, and perfect because it is missing no longer."

This sounds very persuasive and indeed dramatic. A creationist response would initially be that it was a mosaic fish, that it was created and designed for a particular role and having a combination of organs normally found in different body plans - much like the platypus. These organs are fully developed and are not themselves transitional. As Sarfati says:

> When analyzed in detail, the evidence is consistent not with evolution, but with a particular form of intelligent design.... *the biotic message theory*, as proposed by Walter ReMine in The Biotic Message. That is, the evidence from nature points to a *single* designer, but with a pattern which thwarts evolutionary explanations. In this case, the common modules point to *one* common designer, but evolution is powerless to explain this modular pattern, since natural selection can work only on *organisms as a whole*. That is, it cannot select for particular head design as such, but only for *creatures* that have a head that confers superior fitness. But a designer who worked with different modules could create different creatures with different modules, that fit no consistent evolutionary pattern.[146]

A creationist would as well reject the time scale involved (more on that later). Another discovery has refuted the claim for Tiktaalik's ancestral status - even within the evolutionary framework. Tiktaalik was discovered in 2006. In 2009 a discovery was made in Poland of lizard tracks dated by the evolutionary timescale as coming from 10 million years *before* Tiktaalik. As reported in *Nature* this has enormous significance. The abstract in part reads:

> Here we present well-preserved and securely dated tetrapod tracks from Polish marine tidal flat sediments of early Middle Devonian (Eifelian stage) age that are approximately 18 million years older than the earliest tetrapod body fossils and 10 million years earlier than the oldest elpistostegids. They force a radical reassessment of the timing, ecology and environmental setting of the fish–tetrapod transition, as well as the completeness of the body fossil record.[147]

The lizard which made the tracks was more than two meters long. From an evolutionary point of view (and simple logic), it is impossible for Tiktaalik to be the ancestor of a fully fledged reptile which preceded it by 10 million years. Again, a creationist would not accept any of these dates but would see the two creatures as contemporaries from pre-Flood times who were overwhelmed in the deluge. If the fresh water environment is correct for Tiktaalik, that can easily be accounted for by the hydrodynamics and ecological zonation of the flood waters (see below).

M. A Brief Summary of Deluge Palaeontology

We have already considered the vast sedimentary strata laid down upon the continents. We have further considered the sorting mechanism of flowing water. Furthermore, one would expect aquatic life to be overwhelmed and buried by the initial sediments of the cataclysm. Amphibians would be next. Reptiles would tend to be lower in the strata than mammals since mammalian bodies tend to be more buoyant than the former. Also, reptiles may have lived closer to the coast than mammals. Birds by definition would tend to be high in the strata, since by reason of flight they could avoid the early onslaughts. Connected with these considerations we have to take into account other aspects of ecological zonation - certain animals gravitate to certain environmental niches. Depending how segregated they were from other animal kinds, their habitats would have been buried in sediments separate from others.

Needless to say, the flood model would predict a 'rough' distribution of fossils with areas of specificity. It also explains the lack of 'intermediate' fossils since they never existed. We are looking at a world that *being overflowed with water, perished.* (2 Peter 3:6)

N. Four Predictions of the Flood Model

There are predictions that can be made on the basis of the Genesis Flood and on the basis of the catastrophic plate tectonics model.

First, we would expect to find massive, continental and semi-continental sedimentary strata containing billions of dead things. This is exactly what we do find.

Second, we would expect to find remembrance of the flood among the peoples of the world independent of specific Christian influence. Though not dealt with in this book, it is a well known phenomenon.[148]

(From the CPT model two specific predictions were made which were verified subsequent to their being written):

Third, there would be a cooler zone at the bottom of the mantle where sub-oceanic pre-flood blocks had settled after their descent. This has subsequently been verified as seen above.

Fourth, there would be rapid reversals of the earth's magnetic field recorded in single lava flows due to large temperature differentials produced by the descending blocks as they came to rest above the outer core. This has been verified as seen above.

O. The Post-Flood Ice Age[149]

At the end of the flood, the oceans would have been substantially warmed by the upwelling of magma from the mid-oceanic ridge system. The world's oceans would be around 30^0 C (similar to today's Caribbean). At the same time, the atmosphere would have a substantially increased cloud cover due to high altitude particles from the massive volcanism that would have accompanied the catastrophic plate movements. These two features are the ideal recipe for an Ice Age.

From whose womb comes the ice?
Who gives birth to the frost from the heavens

when the waters become hard as stone,
when the surface of the deep is frozen? (Job 38:29-30 NIV)

In God's rhetorical questions to Job, he includes a reference to the freezing of the "surface of the deep." The 'deep' (Heb. *T^eH^oM*) has a greater reference than a local pond. Normally it has oceanic overtones. Job's attention is most likely being drawn to a significant glacial phenomenon. During the ice age when much of northern Europe was covered by ice, North Africa and the Levant would have had greater rainfall than at present with much greater vegetation. This and other texts indicate that the patriarchal period was probably during the Ice Age.

Larry Vardiman writes:

Land-use studies throughout the Mediterranean, North Africa, and the Mid East show the prevalence of crops and forests which were suited to cooler, wetter climates in the period before 1000 B.C. (Crowley and North, 1991). Lake levels in North Africa and throughout the Mid East were high during the "Ice Age" compared to today (Street-Perrott and Harrison, 1985). Agriculture and grasslands were common throughout portions of North Africa, which are deserts today. Petroglyphs of giraffes, zebras, and lions grazing in fields of tall grass have been found on rocky outcrops in the middle of the Sahara. Radar imagery from the space ship *Columbia* taken over the Sahara Desert shows river channels with complete tributary systems buried beneath the sand, providing evidence of greater rainfall in the past (Jet Propulsion Laboratory, NASA).

Global computer climate simulations indicate that during the "Ice Age" the climate was dramatically different in North Africa and throughout the Mid East. The ice sheets which covered North America and northern Europe caused the jet stream in the northern hemisphere to move further south forcing the storm tracks to move across North Africa. This more southerly storm track produced a wetter, cooler climate throughout Israel (Kutzbach and Wright, 1985). [150]

The warm oceans would yield substantial evaporation which, during the winters and at higher latitudes and higher altitudes (tops of high mountains), would produce significant snowfall. The summers would be relatively cool because of greater cloud cover, so the snow pack would not completely melt. For a few centuries this would continue and an ice age would develop.

After a number of centuries had passed, the rate of oceanic evaporation would slow down since the process, by definition, had removed heat from the waters. Furthermore, the cloud cover would be diminished as both the atmospheric dust and water vapour would be reduced to more or less current levels. During the Ice Age, the Arctic Ocean would have shared in the global oceanic warmth (though cooler than other oceans), and because of wind currents over the north Asian land mass, Siberia (plus Alaska and northern Canada) would not experience the ice sheet coverage. The land would have been well watered and lush with vegetation. Consequently, as animals spread from the Ark and multiplied, those that migrated to Siberia found a highly hospitable environment. They multiplied greatly, and included large herbivores such as mammoths, and carnivores such as sabre-toothed tigers, and a host of other creatures. Since elephantine animals require enormous amounts of vegetation (grasses) to survive, there must have been sufficient nourishment available as well as good soil and long warm growing seasons.

Modern elephants, whether African or Asian, have reproduction rates that would allow population doubling a minimum of four times a century.[151] This would enable substantial herds to build up in a few hundred years.

A further development would be a dramatic climate change at the end of the Ice Age. Land based ice sheets would start to melt releasing vast amounts of melt water into the Arctic Ocean. Snelling summarizes Oard's analysis:

> Oard points out that much melt-water would also pour onto the ocean. Salt water stays liquid below 0°C (32°F), and is denser than fresh water. So if melt-water poured into the Arctic Ocean, it would tend to float on top, and freeze. The resulting

ice layer would cover much of the ocean's surface. The ice would separate the air from the ocean, and reflect sunlight, preventing it from heating the earth (albedo effect), because this requires absorption of the radiation. Snow would soon fall, increasing the albedo even more. [152]

While the transition was occurring, high velocity winds would be generated causing significant dust storms. In fact, the modern Siberian landscape is replete with vast amounts of loess - wind driven silt mixed with smaller amounts of clay and sand and calcium carbonate ($CaCo_3$). The wide extent of this phenomenon indicates violent winds sweeping across the north Asian land mass. The source of much of this silt may have been left over mud from the Flood as well as from partially exposed continental shelf at the height of the Ice Age.[153] Many of the 'frozen mammoths' etc., were clearly caught in this sudden onslaught of dust storms and temperature drop. Some of the animal remains indicate death by asphyxiation as they fought to survive this double pronged attack. Oard clarifies the time element in a '*TJ* forum' with Malcolm Bowden:

> Besides the other minor burials in river sediments, bogs, etc., the mammoths did not die in one dust storm, but must have been entombed by many dust storms over a period of a few hundred years: 'Dust storms of variable intensity likely blew from time to time for a few hundred years near the end of the ice age.'... There is strong evidence for a great amount of loess deposition. For instance, the thickness of loess is about 10 to 35 m in north central Siberia but around 50 m thick near the Lena and Aldan Rivers of central Siberia. The loess is thickest near the rivers and thins in the uplands, typical of loess deposits elsewhere.
>
> I did not mean to indicate that most of the mammals died in the dust storms themselves. I meant to say that at least **some** mammoths and other mammals were killed by the dust storms, but the vast majority could have been simply buried and preserved by the accumulating dust. Therefore, most of the animals probably died from other causes and their flesh rotted

while being buried in dust. The point is that bones and tusks still have to be buried and interred into the permafrost within say 30 years, or else these would decay. Since many bones and tusks are well preserved, especially in more northerly areas, this means that they were covered by small to moderate dust storms. This is the general case.[154]

Just to emphasize what is being presented here; the Bible gives a history of the world that differs dramatically from that given by the neo-Darwinian synthesis with its billions of years. In the course of that history we have been considering scientific implications of the biblical account. I would submit that even with the brief treatment we have given the preceding topics it is clear that this project is capable of rational defence.

P. THE TOWER OF BABEL

It is estimated that the six thousand or more languages spoken in the world today can be described as members of about twenty 'families'.[155] The word 'about' is used for two reasons. First, the number may be higher if currently more isolated languages (e.g., Basque) should be classed as separate families. Second, the number may be reduced if it is determined that two designated families are in fact one family.[156] The main point about the different 'families' is that all the members of one family (e.g., Indo European) can be traced back to a single language. In turn, that single original language cannot be derived from another language. If there are in fact only twenty 'families,' then at the start point there were only twenty languages.

The origin of language is a puzzle to evolutionists. Linguists recognize that human language is not simply a higher form of animal sounds. The most obvious example is that of language recursion. This refers to the human ability to take two or more phrases or clauses and imbed one in the other or join them together in additive fashion. An example of the former would be the imbedding of "the swiftest of them all" in "the runner reached the city gate" to produce "the runner, the swiftest of them all, reached the city gate." In spite of years of teaching apes to use symbols nothing remotely like this has been observed. Humans do this effortlessly all the time. Additive would be something like "And God saw"+ "that it was good."

The fact that a statement in any language can be translated into any other language indicates that underlying the different language families is a common or basic linguistic structure. This observation counters that of "language mystique" whereby the claim is made that you can only say 'such and such' in a certain language. From the standpoint of linguistics that is simply not the case.

This contrast between the different language families and their underlying grammatical convertibility would strongly imply that there was originally one universal language and that at a moment in time it was broken up into a limited number of languages each with a different vocabulary and grammar.

This seems to flow inexorably from historical and comparative linguistics. K.J. Duursma was perfectly justified in entitling his 2002 article on this topic "The Tower of Babel account confirmed by linguistics."[157]

Furthermore, the Divine division of human race by language would not have involved a random distribution of new tongues. Rather, it would have been along kinship groupings. Certainly, the "Table of Nations" listed in Genesis 10 is described that way. It is stated that the dispersal of the human race was according to their 'clans,' 'lines of descent,' and 'languages.' The first two clearly refer to genetic factors and the third to linguistic. These factors are interchangeable according to the text, informing us that the language division was along family lines.

This explains as well the origin of distinctive 'people groups' with different external characteristics. I use the term 'people group' in place of the word 'race'. There is only one race - the human race. In the popular consciousness there is often the idea that distinguishing ethnic physical features (skin colour, eyelid shape, etc.) must have taken a long time to develop. If, however, we take notice of certain facts, we discover that current people group distinguishing characteristics could have arisen in one or two generations.

First, we recognize that genetic variation is greater within a people group than it is between people groups. For instance, the differences in

DNA between any two people in the world are estimated to be around 0.2%. Only 6% of this difference (0.012%) is due to 'race.' Therefore, 94% (0.188%) is within 'race.'[158] In fact, in 2000, Francis Collins stated at the completion of the Human Genome project, that human genetic differences amounted to about 0.1%, half of the above figure.[159] The 'people group' difference would be correspondingly smaller at 0.006%

Second, Adam and Eve would have had a gene pool capable of producing children exhibiting a wide range of human expression. To be more specific, pictures of our first parents which portray them as Caucasians are false and furthermore, harmful. If you blended the world's population you would probably have a rough approximation of what they looked like - medium brown in complexion, somewhat almond eyed, black hair - a description of what most of the global population looks like.

From Adam to the Tower of Babel the human race spoke the same language. The chronology of Genesis 5 indicates the Flood came approximately 1656 years after the creation of Adam and Eve (See above, 4.I. for the use of approx.) By current standards, one would assume that significantly different dialects, if not different languages, would develop. For example, if an ancestor were to come from 400 A.D. to today, his or her speech would be incomprehensible to a modern person. It is true that some languages have remained more intact than others due to cultural and sometimes geographic isolation. A simple reason that languages change is, among many other factors, our relatively short life spans. From Adam to Babel, however, life spans were much longer and marriage among people would not have been restricted by linguistic barriers.

After the tower of Babel the human race was broken up into (17? see Sforza above) discrete linguistic groups along kinship lines. They subsequently separated and most moved away from Babel. As they migrated they were, in effect, creating a second wave of genetic bottlenecks after the eight person bottleneck of Noah's family. Without constant inter-clan marriage, external characteristics, such as mentioned above, would be distributed differently among different groups.

Some families would have the genetic programming for more melanin than others so their children would be darker skinned, whereas the reverse would be the case for those with less melanin.[160] The same phenomenon would apply to other physical characteristics, which from a genetic standpoint, are relatively trivial.

A factor that puzzles some people is the necessity for consanguine marriages immediately after the creation and after the flood in order to build up the human population. Brother-sister marriages would be at first obligatory and afterwards quite common. We have, however, seen the progressive deterioration of the human genome and the increasing weight of mutational burden. Without the degree of mutational load that would develop later on, the dangers of consanguinity would not be a health issue for our ancestors. Indeed, the prohibitions against close family marriages are first revealed at the time of Moses in Leviticus 18 (15th century B.C.).

A further note regarding genetic deterioration regards the drop from long age spans to current levels. From Adam to Noah the life spans are in the high hundreds of years. Following the Flood the ages begin to drop till eventually they stabilize around 70-80 (Psalm 90:10). A possible explanation lies in the shortening of telomeres at chromosomal ends during cell reproduction thus leading to cellular senescence. Though this is held to be a strong possibility for cellular aging, caution must be exercised in concluding it to be the definitive explanation.

Nevertheless, an intriguing observation is that the decline in ages found in Genesis 11 (Noah to Abraham) follows a geometric and not an arithmetic drop. In other words, when the ages of the ten generations are plotted on a graph they form a curve and not a straight line. Thus the decline between two individuals at the beginning of the list is not the same as in the middle or the end. If the list was simply made up by a scribe, the most obvious way to shorten the life spans would be to simply subtract the same amount for each succeeding generation. The fact that it does not do that but follows instead this other kind of decline shows a highly realistic scenario. Decay rates in nature are invariably geometric and not arithmetic.

As Sandford states:

> When Biblical life spans are plotted against time, for the generations after Noah, we see a dramatic decline in life

expectancy with a strong appearance of a biological decay curve. Fitting the data to the "line of best fit" reveals an exponential curve following the formula $y=5029.2x^{-1.4322}$. The curve fits very well, with a correlation coefficient of 0.90. It seems highly unlikely this Biblical data could have been fabricated. The curve is very consistent with the concept of genomic degeneration caused by mutation accumulation.[161]

To sum up this discussion, the genealogical figures in Genesis indicate a natural genetic decay rate - and are perfectly consistent with biological science as we know it today.

Having considered key moments in the biblical account of origins and their scientific implications and having alluded, from time to time to the issue of the age of the world, we will now turn our attention to the issue of deep time.

Introduction to How Old Is Time?

A. Introduction to How Old is Time?

THERE IS NO SCIENTIFIC METHOD THAT CAN, WITH ABSOLUTE ASSURANCE, determine the age of any given object. An object exists in the present and we can make assumptions about how that object or state of affairs came about. We may note some process that seems responsible for producing the object and we may further determine the current rate of the process. Assuming the rate to have been constant throughout time, and having a concept of what the original state of affairs was, we may then hazard a conclusion as to the object's age. In other words, we are taking a current process rate and extrapolating it backwards in time to see how far it goes.

When we considered the difference between operational and historical science we looked at the example of determining the age of zircon crystals. Using two different processes we ended up with an age estimate of either 1.5 billion years or 6000 +/- 33%. Since these ages are six orders of magnitude apart they cannot possibly be "averaged" in any meaningful way. We then had to hypothesize which was more reliable. Since the amount of extrapolation for the egress of helium was a million-fold less than that of the specified nuclear transformation rate it makes more sense to postulate a time of accelerated nuclear decay within the last six thousand years or so.

Creationists have researched and published numerous transformation processes at the terrestrial, solar system, galactic and indeed wider cosmic levels. These processes, when extrapolated back in time invariably indicate an age orders of magnitude less than the purported billions of years evolutionary theory demands. As nuclear physicist D. Russell Humphreys has pointed out:

> I estimate that there are probably several hundred processes that one could use to get an idea of the age of the earth. Only a few dozen, at most, of these processes seem to give you billions of years. The other 90 per cent of those processes give you ages much less than billions of years. So it seems like it would be good science to go with the flow of the 90 per cent of the data, and use as a working hypothesis that the Earth really is young and then to try to find explanations for the other 10 per cent of the data.
>
> That whole process seems to be a much more scientific approach than the one that is taken by evolutionists. Basically, they concentrate on the 10 per cent of the data, and that's the data you've always heard about. Such as the light travelling from distant galaxies and the radiometric dating techniques, and a few other things like that.[162]

These words may be a surprise to many. Most people are under the mistaken impression that the overwhelming weight of scientific evidence favours billions, not thousands, of years. Though a surprise to many, it can be demonstrated quite clearly to be the case.

In fact this line of argument uses a principle of logic known as *reductio ad absurdum*. For purposes of argument, we grant the evolutionary assumption of "the present is the key to the past." This principle was first propounded in modern times by James Hutton (as noted above). The American Museum of Natural History article on Hutton states:

> In a paper presented in 1788 before the Royal Society of Edinburgh, a newly-founded scientific organization, Hutton described a universe very different from the Biblical cosmos: one formed by a continuous cycle in which rocks and soil are washed into the sea, compacted into bedrock, forced up to the surface by volcanic processes, and eventually worn away into

sediment once again. "The result, therefore, of this physical enquiry," Hutton concluded, "is that we find no vestige of a beginning, no prospect of an end."....

Another of Hutton's key concepts was the Theory of Uniformitarianism. This was the belief that geological forces at work in the present day—barely noticeable to the human eye, yet immense in their impact—are the same as those that operated in the past. This means that the rates at which processes such as erosion or sedimentation occur today are similar to past rates, making it possible to estimate the times it took to deposit a sandstone, for example, of a given thickness. It became evident from such analysis that enormous lengths of time were required to account for the thicknesses of exposed rock layers. Uniformitarianism is one of the fundamental principles of earth science. Hutton's theories amounted to a frontal attack on a popular contemporary school of thought called catastrophism: the belief that only natural catastrophes, such as the Great Flood, could account for the form and nature of a 6,000-year-old Earth. The great age of Earth was the first revolutionary concept to emerge from the new science of geology.[163]

This description of Hutton's contribution to geological thought is extremely revealing. We note that the operating assumption in Hutton's mind was that current processes and rates are sufficient to explain all the earth's topography. Thus, his purpose was to overthrow the Biblical account of a recent creation and subsequent deluge. He went as far as positing an eternal earth.

In spite of the AMNH's appreciation of his work, it is readily apparent that he and others (e.g. Playfair and Lyell) did not 'discover' vast eons of time, but rather 'posited' it and then fit the data into it. Uniformatarianism - the present is the key to the past - is a prior philosophical commitment which is not derived from an investigation of the earth but is brought to that investigation. We have already seen, in our discussion of the Flood of Noah, that this principle is woefully inadequate as an interpretive guide to understanding the global sedimentary strata. The resistance to the Biblical account is based, not on scientific grounds, but rather ideological foundations.

Without belabouring this point too much, it clearly demonstrates the falsehood of the claim that these late eighteenth and early nineteenth century geologists were being led by their field studies to reluctantly conclude the Mosaic record to be an erroneous account. In fact they started with an animus against the Bible, made unverifiable assumptions (especially uniformitarianism), which by very definition excluded the possibility of a recent creation and a global deluge. This can hardly be called a scientific approach but rather an approach driven by a 'religious' agenda.

Having made these observations, we will now consider some representative processes which clearly preclude the standard evolutionary time frame - even using uniformitarianism as our method.

B. THE DECAY OF THE EARTH'S MAGNETIC FIELD

One argument for a young earth is the decay of the magnetic field. The source of the magnetic field is in the liquid iron/nickel outer core of the planet. It has often been claimed that it is generated by dynamo motions in this liquid outer core[164] produced by the *Coriolis* effect attendant upon the rotation of the planet. Since the outer core of the earth is an electrically conducting liquid medium, it is posited to be sufficient with the necessary convection currents to function as a dynamo. In turn, this is held to be the explanation for a self-generating magnetic field that can last through billions of years.

This is necessary since, otherwise, the magnetic field (in its dipole component) would not last longer than approximately 15,000 years.[165] In fact, the rapid decay of the field is the rationale adduced for the dynamo - see previous note. This rationale assumes a 4.5 billion year old earth and this assumption can only be acceptable if the magnetic field is of similar duration. Furthermore, no real satisfactory dynamo model has been developed that takes into account all the factors involved. As Richard Fitzpatrick (University of Texas at Austin) comments:

> Dynamo theory involves two vector fields, V and B, coupled by a rather complicated force: *i.e.*, the Lorentz force. It is

Introduction to How Old is Time?

not surprising, therefore, that dynamo theory tends to be extremely complicated, and is, at present, far from completely understood.[166]

A major problem with dynamo theory is that it has failed to accurately estimate the magnetic fields of other planets. Prior to 1986 it was generally assumed that Uranus had a magnetic moment of 10^{19} Amperes/m^2 or none at all.[167] This was based on dynamo theory and an age of 4.5 billion years. When Voyager 2 passed by in January 20, 1986 it was discovered to be 3.0 x10^{24} A/m^2, one hundred thousand times greater than the supposed maximum.

In December of 1984 in the *Creation Research Science Quarterly*, D. Russell Humphreys had made a scientific prediction based on two assumptions. He posited that at creation God had oriented the atoms of the planetary cores in uniform directions. Since each atom is a mini magnet this would initiate an electrical current with a magnetic field. The atoms would begin to randomize in their orientation, the current would decrease, and so would the field. His second assumption was that the planets were only about six thousand years old. His prediction: when Voyager 2 would pass Uranus two years later it would find a magnetic field of 10^{24}.

An illustrative interchange of correspondence ensued as a result. The following is taken from an interview of Humphreys in *Creation Magazine*:

CM So, what was the result when Voyager finally made the measurements?

DRH The result was smack in the middle of my prediction, and 100,000 times greater than the evolutionary predictions. So the creation model was the clear winner in that case.

CM And for Neptune as well.

DRH Yes, that's right.

CM Did you get any comments from evolutionists about these fulfilled predictions?

DRH Yes. Stephen Brush, a fairly well known anti-creationist in the United States, wrote to me after the first prediction came true and I had mentioned this in an ICR Impact article. He said he was basically trying to find some way around the fact that I had made a prediction, and I wrote him a polite letter back and tried to explain things to him. He wrote another letter back and that was the end of the correspondence.

But about six months later, an article by him appeared in Science magazine. The gist of it was that 'Well, predictions are not really a way to do good science', so he was basically backing down from the classical scientific view that predictions are a good way to validate a theory.[168]

Though Humphreys prediction for Neptune was also in the range of 10^{24} amperes/m² this was similar to the dynamo prediction since Neptune gives off more heat than it receives – indicating a hot interior. What the Dynamo theory cannot explain, however, is the fact that for both planets the magnetic fields are 60⁰ off their rotational axes. Furthermore, the source of each planet's magnetic field is offset from the planetary centre by about a third of its diameter. It is to be noted as well that Uranus' rotational axis is close to its orbital plane – totally inconsistent with the standard evolutionary nebular hypothesis. As Humphreys notes:

Neither the creation nor the dynamo theory predicted these features. However, it is much more difficult to explain the tilts and offsets with the dynamo theory than it is with the creation theory. According to the dynamo theory, the magnetic and rotation axes should nearly always be closely aligned, except for a very small fraction of the time when the direction of the field is reversing. Thus, when Voyager passed Uranus, pundits explained that the planet is in the rare act of flipping its magnetic field. However, that explanation became highly unlikely when Neptune's magnetic tilt was discovered. One comment was: "Two odd magnetic fields is one too many."[8] A creationist explanation could involve the field's source being in the planet's *solid* core, which could be displaced by accreted material sinking through the vast outer planetary ocean of fluid. Such a displacement could influence both the magnetic and rotational tilt of the planet.⁹ Dynamo theory cannot consider this possibility because their postulated field-generating mechanism cannot work in a solid.¹⁶⁹

The dynamo theory is further challenged by other planetary and lunar magnetic field discoveries. In particular, the Moon, Mercury and Mars have yielded results consistent with the creationist model but not with the billions of years dynamo theory.¹⁷⁰

A further example is Ganymede, Jupiter's largest moon (about 200 km. larger in radius than Mercury). The Galileo probe orbited Jupiter from 1995-2003. It detected a small magnetic field around Ganymede which was unexpected by dynamo theorists. A paper which seeks to explain how such a dynamo could have formed was written in 2008.¹⁷¹ The authors examined a number of possibilities including compositional convection in which constituent elements of the core (primarily iron and sulphur) separate with the lighter sulphur rising upward and the iron sinking downward. It is thought that this action would release heat and in the process engender convection and a magnetic field. The difficulty is that the cold mantle material would absorb the heat and the motion would cease after an astronomically brief time. The authors recognize the difficulties involved but are, nevertheless, convinced that the long age dynamo model must hold. A 6000 year old solar system is not even a topic of possibility.

On the other hand, the aforementioned creationist model is perfectly consistent with the data.¹⁷²

As one evolutionist has said:
You would have thought we would have given up guessing about planetary magnetic fields after being wrong at nearly every planet in the solar system....¹⁷³

If we consider the actual data we have, it is apparent that the earth's magnetic field cannot be more than 15,000 years old (see Paul Demorest's comments above). The model that Humphreys proposes as the most reasonable theory is 'dynamic decay.'¹⁷⁴ This refers to the fact that there were rapid reversals of the magnetic field during the Flood (see discussion of Catastrophic Plate Tectonics above). During these reversals the decline would accelerate even faster.

Some had argued that though the dipole part of the magnetic field was decaying, the non-dipole parts[175] were increasing at a sufficient rate to compensate for the former's decline. This has been refuted by the most recent data. As Humphreys explains in the abstract of a paper he wrote in 2002:

> This paper closes a loophole in the case for a young earth based on the loss of energy from various parts of the earth's magnetic field. Using ambiguous 1967 data, evolutionists had claimed that energy gains in minor ("non-dipole") parts compensate for the energy loss from the main ("dipole") part. However, nobody seems to have checked that claim with newer, more accurate data. Using data from the International Geomagnetic Reference Field (IGRF) I show that from 1970 to 2000, the dipole part of the field steadily lost 235 ± 5 billion megajoules of energy, while the non-dipole part gained only 129 ± 8 billion megajoules. Over that 30-year period, the net loss of energy from all observable parts of the field was 1.41 ± 0.16 %. At that rate, the field would lose half its energy every 1465 ± 166 years. Combined with my 1990 theory explaining reversals of polarity during the Genesis Flood and intensity fluctuations after that, these new data support the creationist model: the field has rapidly and continuously lost energy ever since God created it about 6,000 years ago.[176]

Thus, the hard data, as well as theoretical considerations, lead to the conclusion that the dynamo theory is a valiant but invalid attempt to preserve faith in a 4.5 billion year old earth and solar system. The alternative creationist theory which is based on classical, established understandings of magnetism has been verified in numerous ways. It is overwhelming evidence to any objective observer that the age of the earth's magnetic field, and thus of the planet itself, is measurable in a biblical time scale and not an evolutionary one.

C. Atmospheric Helium and NASA observations

I have decided to present this issue even though the traditional creationist argument has been recently challenged by critics who cite NASA discoveries. The challenge has validity and the creationist argument must be modified. Nevertheless, significant caveats must be attached to the criticism as will be seen. I find this to be instructive for both sides to consider strong and weak points and to consider all the evidence at hand.

The traditional creationist argument was subdivided into two components. Helium is a by-product of nuclear decay. As such, assuming the earth to be 4.5 billion years old we need to know the rate of entrance of helium from the earth's crust into the atmosphere. Secondly, we need to know the corresponding rate of egress from the atmosphere into the vacuum of space. This will first be presented in its 'classical' form. It will then be followed by recent NASA observations of massive solar ejections and their impact on polar sweeping of atmospheric ionized gases.

The first process to be considered is the rate of helium's release into the atmosphere from the ground. From a variety of sources[177], it has been determined that helium atoms enter the atmosphere at a rate of 2×10^6 $cm^{-2}sec^{-1}$. If this rate has continued for 4.5 billion years then there should be a total of 7.3×10^{18} grams. The actual amount is $3.8 \times 10^{15}gm$[178], 1/2000 of the expected amount. Assuming there was no primordial helium[179] in the atmosphere and that there was never a period of accelerated nuclear decay, it would yield a maximum age of about two million years. Since this is unacceptable to the evolutionary time frame there have been efforts to find out how over 4.3 billion years of helium production has disappeared from the atmosphere.

This leads to the second issue. There is the process of 'Jeans escape.'[180] This refers to a gas molecule's velocity being sufficient to escape a given planet's gravitational pull. It is hoped that this and perhaps other mechanisms may explain this significant discrepancy. Walker describes this in further detail (emphasis his):

> Let us assume that there is a level in the atmosphere, called the **critical level** or **exobase**, above which collisions between molecules are so infrequent as to be negligible and below which collisions are sufficiently frequent to maintain a completely

isotropic and random distribution of molecular velocities. At or below the exobase, therefore, the velocity distribution of the molecules of a given atmospheric constituent is the **Maxwellian distribution**. Since collisions are negligible above the exobase, the molecules in this region, called the **exosphere**, move along ballistic trajectories under the action of the earth's gravitational field. Some of the upward-moving molecules have velocities sufficiently great to carry them on hyperbolic trajectories away from the earth, into space.[181]

The specific formulae for considering the velocity of escape for a gas into space according to Jeans escape is as follows: $V_e = (2GM/r+Z)^{-1/2}$. [V_e =escape velocity; G = gravitational constant - see above; M is the mass of the planet; r is the radius of the planet; Z is the distance from the planet's surface; the molecule's mass is not factored into the equation.] Attempts have been made to actually measure helium's release from the atmosphere to see if increases in exosphere temperatures have been significant enough to accelerate helium's egress from the atmosphere.

'MacDonald (1963, 1964) has evaluated the escape flux averaged over an entire 11-year cycle of solar activity, using satellite data on exospheric temperature. He finds an average escape flux of 6×10^4 $cm^{-2}sec^{-1}$, a factor of 30 less than the source. It is still possible, nevertheless, that the bulk of escape occurs during infrequent periods of unusually high temperature (Spitzer, 1949; Hunten 1973). Hunten has pointed out that if the temperature were to exceed 2000 K, diffusion would become the limiting process and the escape flux would be equal to the limiting flux, about 10^8 $cm^{-2}sec^{-1}$. To provide an average loss rate of $2 \times 10^6 cm^{-2}sec^{-1}$, these hot episodes would therefore have to occupy about 2% of the time.'[182]

As Malcolm points out, these hot episodes would, in theory, solve the problem. Such episodes, however, have never been observed and are theoretically difficult to justify for 2% of evolutionary time - particularly given the 'faint sun' paradox to be noted later. The atmospheric helium assay remains a major difficulty for a 'billions of years' time frame. Malcolm further states:

> To obtain the actual rate of loss of helium, we need to integrate the probability function for all molecules traveling upwards at a speed greater than the escape velocity. This has been done correctly by Walker, and is confirmed by Vardiman.[18] The result is clear:
>
> > The characteristic time for helium escape at an average exospheric temperature of 1500 K is 60 million years[19] or 70 million years[20]. But the magnitude of the source from the decay of radioactive elements has been estimated by a number of researchers[21][22][23][24][25] as 2×10^6 cm^{-2} sec^{-1}. By dividing this flux into the column density of helium in the atmosphere (1.1 $\times 10^{20}$ cm^{-2}) we obtain a residence time for helium of 2 million years, much less than the characteristic escape time.
> >
> > 'This result implies that the rate of Jeans escape at 1500 K is much smaller than the crustal source of helium. Since 1500 K is well above the average temperature of the exosphere, there appears to be a problem with the helium budget of the atmosphere.[26]]
>
> Walker realizes that the influx of helium into the atmosphere vastly outweighs the loss to space by means of Jeans escape. But he is not happy with this result and immediately sets out to suggest various mechanisms that could perhaps account for this obvious problem with orthodox evolutionary science.

At this point it would be helpful to consider some recent criticisms of this line of argument. I take them from an anonymous reviewer ('a customer') of Jonathan Sarfati's *Refuting Evolution*. The review is found on the Amazon website.

> Sarfati (p. 113) also claims that a "lack" of helium escape from the atmosphere supports its "youth." However, recent NASA images show helium and other gases being SWEPT from the Earth's atmosphere into deep space. One event occurred on September 24-25, 1998 after a solar coronal mass emission.

NASA issued a press release regarding the September 24, 1998 event. I quote a substantial portion of it to help us gain a fuller perspective.

Scientists have known since the early 1980s that Earth's upper atmosphere leaks oxygen, helium, and hydrogen ions (atoms that have gained or lost an electron) into space from regions near the poles. But it was not until the Polar spacecraft flew through this fountain of ionized gas in September 1998 that scientists confirmed that the flow of ions was caused by solar activity.

"We now have the first direct, quantifiable evidence that disturbances in the solar wind produce changes in the flow of ions out of the ionosphere," said Dr. Thomas E. Moore of NASA's Goddard Space Flight Center, Greenbelt, MD, principal investigator for Polar's Thermal Ion Dynamics Experiment (TIDE). "This solar wind energy essentially 'cooks' the upper atmosphere off of the Earth." Moore's observations were presented on December 8 in San Francisco, CA, during the fall meeting of the American Geophysical Union.

On September 22, 1998, the Sun ejected a mass of hot, ionized gas (known as plasma) toward Earth. This magnetic cloud of plasma (called a coronal mass ejection) increased the density and pressure of the solar wind and produced a shock wave similar to a sonic boom. When that shock wave arrived at Earth late on September 24, it rammed into and compressed Earth's magnetic shell in space (the magnetosphere). This shock to the magnetosphere excited the plasma trapped in Earth's ionosphere to a point where some ions gained enough energy to escape Earth's gravity and flow downwind of Earth. The amount of oxygen and other gases lost from the ionosphere amounted to a few hundred tons, roughly equivalent to the mass of oxygen inside the Louisiana Superdome.

"This is the supply of plasma that makes things interesting in space," said Moore. "Much of the gas ejected from the ionosphere is caught in Earth's wake. It then flows back toward the Earth while being heated and accelerated by the same processes that create auroral particles and the radiation belts."[183]

The first point to note is that the release of the ionized gases including helium is precipitated by a coronal mass ejection from the sun. This is not a continuous phenomenon. When a solar mass ejection is directed towards or directly away (backside of the sun) from the earth it is called a halo CME since, to an observer on earth, it forms a circle around the sun. Montana State University Department of Solar Physics has a Q&A section that includes the following:[184]

Q: How often do halo CMEs occur?

A: That depends on the phase of the *solar cycle*. The Sun's activity is not the same year after year, but waxes and wanes in a cycle that lasts about eleven years on average. For example, the years 1990-1991, and 2000-2001 saw a large amount of activity (*solar maximum*: many flares and CMEs), whereas 1995-1996 was a time of minimal activity.

According to researchers using data from the SOHO solar observatory satellite, 25 Earth-directed halo CMEs were detected during the last eight months of 1997, and yet ten years later in 2007 there was again a time of low activity. But the fact that the Sun's activity is cyclic means that in the next 1-2 years we should expect to see CMEs becoming more frequent.

Apart from frequency, the issue of amount arises. According to NASA, the amount of oxygen and other gases released from the ionosphere is roughly a few hundred tons which they liken to the amount of atmosphere in the Louisiana Astrodome. Furthermore, they point out that much of it returns to the earth's ionosphere due to the earth's wake. On their diagram (not seen here) they show oxygen returning with the lighter H and He continuing on into space. Considering the faint sun paradox, (see 5. J. below) when, according to long age views, solar energy (for the first billion or so years) was less than today, CMEs would also have been less in number. Furthermore, we know there is a connection between sun spot activity and CME production. NASA notes regarding the variations in solar activity:

Early records of sunspots indicate that the Sun went through a period of inactivity in the late 17th century. Very few sunspots were seen on the Sun from about 1645 to 1715. Although the observations were not as extensive as in later years, the Sun was in fact well observed during this time and this lack of sunspots is well documented. This period of solar inactivity also corresponds to a climatic period called the "Little Ice Age" when rivers that are normally ice-free froze and snow fields remained year-round at lower altitudes. There is evidence that the Sun has had similar periods of inactivity in the more distant past. The connection between solar activity and terrestrial climate is an area of ongoing research.[185]

There are other minima recorded since 1010 A.D.: Oort (1010-1080), Wolf (1280-1350), Sporer (1460-1550), Maunder (1645-1715) and Dalton [not as pronounced as the others] (1790-1850)[186]. Currently we are in the Modern Maximum 1950 – present. It is clear that in addition to the lows and highs of the 11 year solar cycle there are extended periods of low sunspot activity and thus of CMEs. The reason this impacts our discussion is that sunspot activity precipitates CMEs. K.B. Ramesh states:

> Recent studies have indicated that the occurrence of the maxima of coronal mass ejection (CME) rate and sunspot number (SSN) were nearly two years apart. We find that the two-year lag of CME rate manifests only when the SSN index is considered and the lag is minimal (two-three months) when the sunspot area is considered. CMEs with speeds greater than the average speed follow the sunspot cycle much better than the entire population of CMEs. Analysis of the linear speeds of CMEs further indicates that during the descending phase of the solar cycle the loss of magnetic flux is through more frequent and less energetic CMEs. We emphasize that the magnetic field attaining the nonpotentiality that represents the free energy content, rather than the flux content as measured by the area of the active region, plays an important role in producing CMEs.[187]

Since sunspot activity has long term variability including extended periods of quiescence the most reasonable conclusion is that CMEs share the same pattern. Thus to extrapolate back in time from the modern maximum and claim a state of equilibrium for atmospheric helium is unwarranted.

Conclusion: To repeat, the verifiable, measured rates, including the NASA observations, indicate the atmosphere unlikely to be billions of years old. What the NASA data does show is that the previously argued creationist (*reductio ad absurdum* 'uniformitarian') maximum cannot be pegged at 2,000,000 years. So neither the evolutionary time span nor the 2,000,000 year maximum can be maintained. However, it could still be actually 6000 years if God supplied the newly created atmosphere with primordial helium and if there were one or two periods of accelerated nuclear decay episodes in earth history.

D. Blood and Organic Tissue Remains in Dinosaurs

This topic has been the subject of considerable debate for obvious reasons. The presence of still flexible organic remains from dinosaurs, including blood cells and complex proteins, has enormous implications. It is known that complex life molecules and tissues cannot last for any great length of time. Specifically, they cannot last more than a few thousand years - certainly not 65,000,000 years.

There are three issues to consider. First, have haemoglobin, complex proteins and flexible dinosaur tissue been discovered? Second, if so, is it certain that they cannot last 65,000,000 years? Third, if the answer to the first two questions is affirmative, then what are the implications for the dating of the cretaceous strata and indeed of the entire phanerozoic column?

We will first cite the abstract of a major paper published in *Science*, the official publication of the American Association for the Advancement of Science (May 1, 2009):

> Molecular preservation in non-avian dinosaurs is controversial. We present multiple lines of evidence that endogenous proteinaceous material is preserved in bone fragments and soft tissues from an 80-million-year-old Campanianhadrosaur, *Brachylo-*

phosaurus canadensis [Museum of the Rockies (MOR) 2598]. Microstructural and immunological data are consistent with preservation of multiple bone matrix and vessel proteins, and phylogenetic analyses of *Brachylophosaurus* collagen sequenced by mass spectrometry robustly support the bird-dinosaur clade, consistent with an endogenous source for these collagen peptides. These data complement earlier results from *Tyrannosaurus rex* (MOR 1125) and confirm that molecular preservation in Cretaceous dinosaurs is not a unique event.[188]

Furthermore, it must be remembered that the study of this fossil was conducted at several independent labs. Quite a number of soft-tissue structures were discovered. Also present were proteins such as collagen, elastin, and hemoglobin. In addition, the star shaped osteocytes produced from bone forming osteoblasts were present.

The abstract states that hadrosaur remains are 80,000,000 years old. The specimen contains protein molecules which are native to the remains and not a later intrusion. Fine structures and immunological testing indicates actual bone and not simply mineral substitutes. As noted, proteins from vessels (e.g. blood vessels) have been indicated. Collagen (a complex structural protein necessary for bone tissue integrity) has been detected by mass spectrometry and these sophisticated peptides are again seen to be endogenous (native to the sample.) Furthermore, phylogenetic analysis of the collagen affirms a bird-dinosaur connection. Finally these findings confirm previously published[189] molecular evidence from 65,000,000 year old Tyrannosaurus Rex remains.

Two years previous (in 2007) two papers were published by Schweitzer *et al* on a Tyrannosaurus rex as well as a mastodon.[190] Collagen had also been discovered in the T-rex as well as other organic features.

Regarding the bird-dinosaur connection, this has become something of a conviction among a number of researchers (birds as modern dinosaurs). They note that when stretches of the collagen protein were sequenced, the Tyrannosaurus sample was seen to be 58% similar to that of a chicken and 51% similar to a newt and a frog. This is hardly the 'robust' support for the bird-dinosaur clade[191] since when human collagen is sequenced it shows an 81% similarity with that of a frog.[192]

It is clear from this and other research that biological material has been retrieved from dinosaur remains. Their skeletons have not been completely permineralized.

The issue of how this affects dating can be illustrated by the example of collagen. Just how long collagen can last had been addressed in a 1999 article by J. Bada et al.

"....in bones, hydrolysis [breakdown] of the main protein component, collagen, is even more rapid and little intact collagen remains after only $1\text{-}3 \times 10^4$ [10,000 to 30,000] years, except in bones in cool or dry depositional environments."[193]

It was universally accepted, on the basis of laboratory analysis, as well as research on chemical kinetics, that complex three-dimensionally folded life molecules simply could not last in animal remains for millions of years.

An attempt was made to dismiss Schweitzer's original findings on the basis that she had really discovered biofilm residues - which was at first glance a possibility, based on previous results.[194]

The kinds of tests and rigorous analyses conducted by her and her fellow researchers have nullified that possibility. Brian Thomas summarizes the case of the original Tyrannosaurus study (1997 see endnote #163) before the most recent discovery noted above.

First, collagen protein sequence data is not a bacterial product, but "colleagues at Harvard successfully sequenced the dinosaur protein that Schweitzer had extracted from the tissue, identifying the amino acids and confirming that the material from the T. rex was collagen. 'From a paleo standpoint, sequence data really is the nail in the coffin that confirms the preservation of these tissues,' Schweitzer says." [6]

Second, as Dr. Schweitzer pointed out for National Geographic, no biofilms have been observed with hollow, branching tubes. Third, biofilms would have been thicker at the bottom, pulled down by gravity.[7] And fourth, the flimsy biofilms themselves could never have retained the shape of the original dinosaur blood vessels, to which they allegedly conformed, for 68 million years.

Not only should the unfossilized bone and its collagen have turned to dust long ago, but there should certainly be no vestige of blood vessels, or even bacterial slime still shaped like vessels.[195]

Thus it is apparent, on objective scientific grounds, that fresh and flexible organic life tissues, highly complex three dimensionally folded life proteins, blood cells with haemoglobin, and fresh bone have been discovered in various dinosaur remains.

It is further evident that such discoveries indicate the bones cannot possibly be millions of years old but thousands.

The question then arises as to how evolutionists respond to this evidence. Initially, the response was to deny the conclusions - since it was known to be impossible for such life material to be preserved for millions of years. Then as the evidence became conclusive, it was decided that decay rates had been greatly exaggerated - in spite of the aforementioned knowledge of chemical kinetics and laboratory observations. A few paragraphs from a Smithsonian Institute article bring this out in rather clear terms (note the references to creationists, God, faith etc.):

Young-earth creationists also see Schweitzer's work as revolutionary, but in an entirely different way. They first seized upon Schweitzer's work after she wrote an article for the popular science magazine Earth in 1997 about possible red blood cells in her dinosaur specimens. Creation magazine claimed that Schweitzer's research was "powerful testimony against the whole idea of dinosaurs living millions of years ago. It speaks volumes for the Bible's account of a recent creation."

This drives Schweitzer crazy. Geologists have established that the Hell Creek Formation, where B. rex was found, is 68 million years old, and so are the bones buried in it. She's horrified that some Christians accuse her of hiding the true meaning of her data. "They treat you really bad," she says. "They twist your words and they manipulate your data." For her, science and religion represent two different ways of looking at the world; invoking the hand of God to explain natural phenomena breaks the rules of science. After all, she says, what God asks is faith, not evidence. "If you have all this evidence and proof positive that God exists, you don't need faith. I think he kind of designed it so that we'd never be able to prove his existence. And I think that's really cool."

By definition, there is a lot that scientists don't know, because the whole point of science is to explore the unknown. By being clear that scientists haven't explained everything, Schweitzer leaves room for other explanations. "I think that we're always wise to leave certain doors open," she says.[196]

Note the dogmatic assumption: geologists have established the Hell Creek Formation to be 68,000,000 years old and so are the bones buried in it. We have to leave certain doors open. Yet the professed scientific openness to "other explanations" rules out of court the possibility of a radically reduced time frame for geological history.

I do not deny her Christianity but I am puzzled by her comments about her data being manipulated. The articles on CMI, AIG and ICR all accurately reported her findings and drew reasonable conclusions. I have read no aspersions on her motives or character on any of these three major creationist sites. If from some other circles such things were said, it is unfortunate and lacking in grace.

The fact remains that the presence of highly degradable biological phenomena in dinosaur remains is a compelling argument for thousands and not millions of years. No special pleading or ad hoc explanations about disintegration rates need to be employed.

The Biblical presentation that dinosaurs were created along with Adam, that young representatives were on the Ark, and that they multiplied and spread throughout the world after the deluge is perfectly consistent with biological decay rates as well as biblical and many cultural writings and inscriptions attest. Furthermore, it precludes the host strata (in this case cretaceous) from being anything other than a few thousand years old and most probably being laid down by the raging waters of the Great Flood.

E. Excursus: Post Flood Dinosaurs

As mentioned above (in 4. J.) the Bible and cultures around the world refer to reptilian creatures strongly resembling dinosaurs. It may be of interest to consider just a few of these references.

The first we will consider is a brass engraving on Bishop Richard Bell's tomb in Carlisle Cathedral. Bell was born in 1410 and died in 1476. A narrow brass fillet runs around the tomb's top which is level with the floor. The artist engraved animals on the brass e.g., fish, eels, pigs, weasels. He was clearly portraying animals that he had seen and were part of his natural world. On one part of the fillet he engraved what, to any unbiased viewer, are two sauropods either courting or in combat:

http://creation.com/images/creation_mag/vol25/bishop_behemoths_lg.jpg

> Philip Bell comments:
> Bishop Bell's tomb shows the clear signs of heavy wear and tear after several centuries of shuffling feet. Skeletons of dinosaurs have been accurately reconstructed only in the last 100 years or so. Prior to this, scientists classifying these reptiles incorrectly pieced together their bones making the first artistic representations wildly inaccurate. It seems highly improbable that an artist in the 15th century accurately portrayed a creature

Introduction to How Old is Time?

which he had never seen. Rather, it is more likely that these renditions were all creatures which had been observed. Clearly, the only reason modern researchers would fail to identify them as dinosaurs is their antibiblical bias that humans and dinosaurs did not co-exist.[197]

A second engraving is more difficult to identify but it possibly represents an Eryops- an amphibian supposedly thriving during the Permian period approximately 270 million years ago. This, however, is not as evident as the sauropods. Some would say that these gigantic creatures could not have lived in Britain at the time of the artist or they would be reported by many scribes and artists. In response it can be stated that there are numerous early and medieval European references to 'dragons' which are not presented in a fanciful way but as simply part of the animal kingdom - albeit somewhat dangerous. Furthermore, they may not have been all that massive since a huge dinosaur means an old dinosaur. Since reptiles never stop growing, by definition an old dinosaur would be a large one (unless there were other constraints, biological or environmental).

Another example is a North American Anasazi Indian petroglyph of what clearly is a sauropod dinosaur:

http://www.answersingenesis.org/articles/2011/03/18/feedback-senter-and-cole

Origins and Redemption

The Anasazi lived in what is now Utah from ca. 150 B.C. to ca. 1200 A.D. This petroglyph is recognized as genuine by evolutionists since the glyph is coated by brownish hardened desert varnish which is pitted and weathered - thus indicating its age (see above cited website for details). Even evolutionists such as Sentner and Cole who have examined it and yet reject its implications have concluded it is not a forgery. However, it is not a dinosaur at all but a meaningless composite piece of rock art.[198] Though they make a persuasive argument I believe it has more than adequately been responded to by Abrahams.[199]

A third example is taken from a Jewish synagogue dated 400 - 700 A.D. found at Umm El-Kanatir on the Golan. It shows a large unidentified creature (looking somewhat feline) attacking a horse while a small (i.e. young) theropod is about to join the action. One can note what appears to be the dinosaur's thick tail curled up his back. The theropod has a crest on its head as did Cryolophosaurus and Dilophosaurus, two crested theropod dinosaurs. Once again the artist must have seen these creatures in the first millenium A.D.

We have seen three examples of artists representing dinosaurs, clearly indicating that they were contemporary. There are a vast number of others that could be cited. This comports well with the biblical account of creation and the deluge. It does not require the mental gymnastics obligated by separating humans and dinosaurs by 65 million years.

F. The Ubiquity of Carbon 14 in Phanerozoic Strata and in Diamonds

The presence of ^{14}C throughout the fossil bearing strata is a major indicator of recent deposition of the sediments. This is due to the short half-life of the isotope - such that it would not be expected to last much more than 100,000 years. Thus the entire fossil record, the geological column from Proterozoic to Cenozoic, must be less than 100,000 years old. This argument will be presented in the following paragraphs.

We will first start by examining ^{14}C's formation and its decay rate.

^{14}C is an unstable isotope formed when a nitrogen atom is hit by a free neutron travelling at high speeds. In the atmosphere, it is incoming cosmic radiation (protons) that dislodges neutrons from atoms in the

Introduction to How Old is Time?

upper layers. These neutrons, in turn, impact atmospheric nitrogen, ^{14}N, converting it to ^{14}C. Specifically, ^{14}N contains 7 protons and 7 neutrons. The impacting neutron is added to the nucleus and drives out a proton. Thus the nucleus now has 8 neutrons and 6 protons and is now an unstable carbon isotope.[200] This carbon isotope, due to its instability, begins to transform back into ^{14}N by beta⁻ (ß⁻) decay in which a neutron decays into a proton, an electron and electron antineutrino. The rate at which it decays (transforms) is exponential with a half-life of 5730 +/- 30 years. Thus, in that amount of time half the original ^{14}C will have changed back into ^{14}N. The short half life of ^{14}C can be illustrated by the simple fact that if the entire globe consisted of ^{14}C it would all be changed to ^{14}N in less than a million years.[201]

The newly formed carbon isotope quickly unites with oxygen to form CO_2, a gas which makes up 0.039 % of the atmosphere. In turn, the CO_2 with ^{14}C represents about one in a trillion carbon dioxide molecules. Plants and animals contain atmospheric CO_2 to varying degrees. The ^{14}C component is assumed to be the same percentage as found in the atmosphere - a perfectly reasonable assumption reinforced by laboratory analyses of known recent samples.

When the organism dies it no longer cycles the carbon dioxide. Thus the ^{14}C continues to decay with no replacement. Assuming the ^{14}C atmospheric assay to have been in equilibrium throughout geological time it is simply a question of discovering the sample's current $^{14}C/^{12}C$ ratio in order to determine how long the sample has been dead.

Since the 1950's there has been a constant registering of ^{14}C dates in samples which by other methods have been determined to be millions of years old. These samples should be "carbon14 dead." Often this was ignored and explained away as the result of background radiation. This was on the basis that the dating technique measured *beta-decay* events to determine the amount of ^{14}C present. Nevertheless, no matter how many safeguards were employed virtually every specimen showed the presence of radiocarbon. Whitelaw in 1970[202] surveyed the over 15,000 samples recorded in the journal <u>Radiocarbon</u> up to 1970. He discovered that:

All such matter is found datable within 50,000 years as published.

Baumgardner observes:
The samples included coal, oil, natural gas, and other allegedly ancient material. The reason these anomalies were not taken seriously is because the earlier ß-decay counting technique that counted actual ^{14}C decay events had difficulty distinguishing genuine low intrinsic levels of ^{14}C in the samples from background counts due to cosmic rays. The low ^{14}C levels measured in samples that, according to their location in the geological record, ought to have been ^{14}C-dead were therefore simply attributed to the cosmic ray background.[203]

In the 1980's the Accelerated Mass Spectrometry technique became employed. This involves a highly sophisticated machine which literally counts the individual atoms. In spite of this, ^{14}C is consistently found well above detection thresholds. The documentation for this is overwhelming. The only reasonable conclusion is the samples are less than 100,000 years old no matter where their source is on the geological column. Baumgardner again:
However, in samples with uniformitarian ages between one and 500 million years, the peer-reviewed radiocarbon literature documents scores of examples of $^{14}C/C$ ratios in the range 0.1-0.5 percent of the modern $^{14}C/C$ ratio. The lower limit of this range is a factor of ten above the threshold of most AMS laboratories in the world. Another noteworthy observation is that the $^{14}C/C$ of these samples appears to be uncorrelated with their position in the geological record. RATE's own measurement of ^{14}C levels in ten coal samples using one of the world's best AMS laboratories strongly confirms this reported range in $^{14}C/C$ ratio and the lack of dependence of this ratio on position in the rock record. In terms of ^{14}C age, if one takes the assumption, as is normally done, that the $^{14}C/C$ in these fossilized organisms when they died was close to that of

today's atmosphere, the range in ratio of 0.1-0.5 percent of the modern value corresponds to ^{14}C ages between 44,000 and 57,000 years. A straight forward but startling inference from these AMS data is that all but the very youngest fossil material in the geological record was buried contemporaneously only thousands of years ago in what must have been a major global cataclysm. The simultaneous destruction of so much life implies, however, that dramatically more carbon (now in the form of coal, oil and oil shale) had to be present in the earth's biosphere prior to this cataclysmic event. In this case using today's atmospheric ^{14}C/C as the initial ^{14}C/C ratio for this fossil material almost certainly would be a proper assumption. Using a lower, more realistic estimate for the biospheric ^{14}C/C ratio prior to this cataclysm reduces the actual ^{14}C age by roughly a factor of ten from about 50,000 years to a value of about 5000 years. This latter age estimate, of course, is consistent with the Biblical account of a global flood that destroyed most of the life on the planet, both plants and animals, in a single brief cataclysm some four to five millennia ago.[204]

Baumgardner provides a table[205] in which he lists ninety AMS measurements on samples considered to be in excess of one hundred thousand years old. Full documentation is given. It is apparent that ^{14}C when fully considered, yields data eminently in favour of the creationist position and in total contrast to the evolutionary time scale without reference to *ad hoc*, special pleading.

We will next consider the presence of ^{14}C in diamonds. This was a major discovery of the RATE project and further demonstrates the pattern we have already observed.

Diamonds are found deep in the earth and are not exposed to the atmosphere during their formation. This does not prevent the appearance of ^{14}C since the necessary conditions for its production in diamonds are present. Diamonds universally contain nitrogen impurities. Secondly, there is radiation in the earth's mantle and crust.

The presence of carbon 14 in diamonds presents a major evidence for a recent creation and conversely, a major difficulty for billions of years. The reasoning is quite simple. First, we will consider their formation and putative age. Second, we will apply the above mentioned decay rate of C^{14} to the topic. Third, we will consider the age implications.

First, diamonds are formed from carbon under great pressure - the kind of pressure (45- 60 kilobars) found 100-200 kilometres below the surface of the earth. The temperature at this depth in the mantle ranges from $900^0 - 1300^0$ C. Diamonds are shot to the surface through volcanic activity. They are held to be at least 990,000,000 years old with many said to be 3.2 billion years old. [206]

It has been common for decades to produce diamonds artificially using high pressure and heat. Recently the production of pure polycrystalline diamonds from graphite under elevated pressure and temperatures (2300-2500 C) were reported in *Nature*.[207] Though this particular process formed the diamonds in only a few minutes, others have taken longer - often a few months. Given the incredible heat and pressures in the mantle zone of 100-200 kilometres down, it is apparent that natural diamond formation is extremely rapid and does not take eons of time.

Regarding the diamonds in question, they all showed ^{14}C well above detection thresholds. Six African diamonds were chosen: one from a kimberlite pipe (Kimberly) South Africa, four from kimberlite pipes in Botswana [two from the Orapa mine, two from the Letlhakane mine] and one from an alluvial deposit in Guinea.[208] Given the half-life of 5730 years, the diamonds had an average age of 55,700 years using the evolutionary, uniformitarian assumptions. This clearly places the formation of these diamonds in the last few thousand - not billions - of years.

Four objections of a technical nature have been made against the diamond discoveries. Dr. Jonathan Sarfati has responded to them in detail and they will now be presented in verbatim. The objections are underlined.

Introduction to How Old is Time?

G. Excursus: Jonathan Sarfati responds to diamond critics[209]

The ^{14}C readings in the diamonds are the result of background radiation in the detector. This shows that the objector doesn't even understand the method. AMS doesn't measure radiation but counts atoms. It was the obsolete scintillation method that counted only decaying atoms, so was far less sensitive. In any case, the mean of the ^{14}C/C ratios in Dr. Baumgardner's diamonds was close to 0.12±0.01 pMC, well above that of the lab's background of purified natural gas (0.08 pMC).

The ^{14}C was produced by U-fission (this was an excuse proposed for ^{14}C in coal, also analysed in Dr. Baumgardner's paper, but not possible for diamonds). But to explain the observed ^{14}C, then the coal would have to contain 99% uranium, so colloquial parlance would term the sample 'uranium' rather than 'coal'.[1]

The ^{14}C was produced by neutron capture by ^{14}N impurities in the diamonds. But this would generate less than one ten-thousandth of the measured amount even in best case scenarios of normal decay. And as Dr Paul Giem points out:

'One can hypothesize that neutrons were once much more plentiful than they are now, and that is why there is so much carbon-14 in our experimental samples. But the number of neutrons required must be over a million times more than those found today, for at least 6,000 years; and every 5,730 years that we put the neutron shower back doubles the number of neutrons required. Every time we halve the duration of the neutron shower we roughly double its required intensity. Eventually the problem becomes insurmountable. In addition, since nitrogen-14 captures neutrons 110,000 times more easily than does carbon-13, a sample with 0.000 0091% nitrogen should have twice the carbon-14 content of a sample without any nitrogen. If neutron capture is a significant source of carbon-14 in a given sample, radiocarbon dates should vary wildly with the nitrogen content of the sample. I know of no such data. Perhaps this effect should be looked for by anyone

107

seriously proposing that significant quantities of carbon-14 were produced by nuclear synthesis in situ.'[2]

Also, if atmospheric contamination were responsible, the entire carbon content would have to be exchanged every million years or so. But if this were occurring, we would expect huge variations in radiocarbon dates with porosity and thickness, which would also render the method useless.[1] Dr. Baumgardner thus first thought that the ^{14}C must have been there right from the beginning. But if nuclear decay were accelerated, say a recent episode of 500 million years worth, it could explain some of the observed amounts. Indeed, his RATE colleagues have shown good evidence for accelerated decay in the past, which would invalidate radiometric dating.

<u>The ^{14}C 'dates' for the diamonds of 55,700 years were still much older than the biblical timescale.</u> This misses the point: we are not claiming that this 'date' is the actual age; rather, if the earth were just a million years old, let alone 4.6 billion years old, there should be no ^{14}C at all! Another point is that the 55,700 years is based on an assumed ^{14}C level in the atmosphere. Since no one, creationist or evolutionist, thinks there has been an exchange of carbon in the diamond with the atmosphere, using the standard formula for ^{14}C dating to work out the age of a diamond is meaningless. Also, ^{14}C dating assumes that the ^{14}C/C ratio has been constant. But the Flood must have buried huge numbers of carbon-containing living creatures, and some of them likely formed today's coal, oil, natural gas and some of today's fossil-containing limestone. Studies of the ancient biosphere indicate that there was several hundred times as much carbon in the past, so the ^{14}C/C ratio would have been several hundred times smaller. This would explain the observed small amounts of ^{14}C found in 'old' samples that were likely buried in the Flood.

Rotta, R.B., "Evolutionary explanations for anomalous radiocarbon in coal?" *Creation Research Society Quarterly* 41, no. 2 (September 2004): 104-112.

INTRODUCTION TO HOW OLD IS TIME?

Giem, P., "Carbon-14 content of fossil carbon," *Origins* 51 (2001); 6-30, www.grisda.org/origins/51006.htm[210]

It is thus apparent that ^{14}C is a friend of the biblical time scale and a foe of the evolutionary one.

H. DISPARATE RADIOACTIVE "DATES"
This line of evidence is not so much an indicator of a Biblical time frame as it is a serious questioning of confidence in radioactive dating. In chapter 3 we looked at the orders of magnitude difference between $^{238}U \rightarrow ^{206}Pb$ and helium retention "dates." The most reasonable conclusion was that there had been one or two episodes of accelerated nuclear decay. The above mentioned R.A.T.E. project undertook a study of different radioactive methods applied to the same rock samples. The result was that none of the putative dates agreed. The studies were based on samples taken from the Grand Canyon.[211] One of the sample rock systems was an amphibolite layer.

> Among these volcanic layers are distinctive dark-coloured rocks called amphibolites. These were once flows of basalt lava, up to tens of metres thick. Some outcrops reveal round pillow structures, showing that the basalt lavas erupted under water.[212]

A total of 27 samples were taken. The potassium-argon (K-Ar) method yielded calculated 'ages' ranging from 405.1 +/- 10 Ma (million years ago) to 2,574.2 +/- 73 Ma. This is a rather stunning six-fold range of 'dates' for samples taken from lava flows which must have taken place close in time to each other. A specific subset of seven samples from a small amphibolite outcrop which represents a single metamorphosed basalt lava flow had K-Ar 'ages' from 1,060.4 +/- 28 Ma to 2,574.2 +/- 73 Ma. Two samples 0.84 m apart had calculated ages of 1,205.3 +/- 31 and 2,574.2 +/- 73 Ma.

It is clear that the K-Ar method is simply measuring isotopic ratios - a purely physical phenomenon which has absolutely nothing to do with determining the age of a rock sample.

It is often held that the isochron[213] method yields reliable results. Yet difficulties which would nullify its practitioners' confident claims have often been ignored. In the R.A.T.E. study of the same rock formation three isochron methods were employed: rubidium-strontium (Rb-Sr), samarium-neodymium (Sm-Nd) and lead-lead (Pb-Pb). As Andrew Snelling states:

> It is important to note that geologists routinely use only 6–10 samples for plotting isochrons and calculating isochron ages, so the isochrons obtained here from 19–21 samples are exceptional. Furthermore, all the results not included in the isochron 'age' calculations still plotted very close to the lines of best fit.[214]

The result for Rb-Sr was 1240 +/- 84 Ma from 19 of the 27 samples.[215] For the Sm-Nd isochron it was 1,655 ± 40 Ma from 21 samples. The ^{212}Pb-^{208}Pb isochron gave an 'age' of 1,883 ± 53 Ma from 20 samples. Once again, these results are mutually incompatible.

Thus far we have considered only the amphibolite outcrop. Other rock systems were similarly tested and showed equally disparate 'ages.' An example is the diabase sill of the Grand Canyon. This formation showed a K-Ar whole rock isochron of 841.5 +/-164 Ma. The same formation yielded a Sm-Nd mineral isochron age of 1379 +/-140 Ma. Again, we see two radically different dates. If only one of them was recorded it would be said that radio isotope dating has shown the diabase sill to be - take your pick - 841 Ma or 1379 Ma. In actual fact it's neither. Stephen Austin, Ph.D., records other similar discrepancies in his article "Do Radioisotope Clocks Need Repair? Testing the Assumptions of Isochron Dating Using K-Ar, Rb-Sr, Sm-Nd, and Pb-Pb Isotopes."[216]

A rather extreme example of disparate dating is the ten year debate on how to fix a date for the hominid skull KNM-ER 1470[217] discovered by Richard Leakey. At first, K-Ar analysis of the local volcanic KBS (Kay Behrensmeyer Site) Tuff was conducted prior to the discovery of KNM-ER 1470. F.J. Fitch (Birkbeck College, University of London) and J.A. Miller (Cambridge University), well regarded specialists in K-Ar dating, were given a rock sample by Richard Leakey. They determined an age of 212 - 230 million years. Taking into account associated hominid remains and artifacts they concluded that extraneous excess argon accounted for the excessive 'age'. The fossils told them the date was impossible - australopithecine remains below the tuff told them the rocks had to be between 2 and 5 Ma.[218] Receiving fresh samples they determined the age to be 2.61 Ma.[219] Since skull 1470 was found below the Tuff and above rock dated at 3.18 Ma, Leakey calculated the age to be 2.9 Ma. Marvin Lubenow gives an overview of the dating of the KBS environs:[220]

> In 1972, before skull 1470 was announced, Vincent Maglio (Princeton University) published in *Nature* a chronology of the hominid-bearing sediments east of Lake Rudolf, included the KBS Tuff.[4] His work was based on lineages of two species of **pig** and one of **elephant**. Maglio's dates were compatible with the radiometric date arrived at by Fitchand Miller, and were considered to confirm their date.
>
> In 1974, a third chronology of the area was published in *Nature*, based on palaeomagnetism.[5] The conclusion of 2.7 to 3.0 million years seemed to represent a 'bulls-eye' for the correlation of the various dating methods.[6]
>
> By late 1974, the KBS Tuff had been dated five different times by four different dating methods. The alleged compatibility of the different methods would seem to be a geologist's dream.

The date of 2.9 Ma did not last in spite of the agreement of different techniques. The reason was that Leakey's 2.9 Ma age for such a modern looking skull as 1470 was simply unacceptable to evolutionary palaeontologists. Lubenow continues:

> On March 20, 1980, two more dating studies in *Nature* criticized the earlier work and claimed that the age of the KBS Tuff was 1.87 or 1.89 million years. Then in late 1981, Ian McDougall published his study of the KBS Tuff, giving a date of 1.88 million years. At that point, the 10-year controversy over the date of the KBS Tuff came to a close with agreement on the more recent date.[221]

The conclusion from all of this is that radiometric dating is not as objective as is often claimed. Dates do differ on the same sample. One suspects that there is an unconscious (or conscious) desire to confirm the 'preferred' or 'expected' date - based on evolutionary assumptions.

Actually, it was a 1975 study of pig evolution that provided the impetus for redating the site.

Donald Johanson tells of attending the 1975 Bishop Conference on anthropology and geology in London. A major paper was presented by Basil Cooke (Dalhousie University, Halifax), who had studied the pig sequences in southern Ethiopia, at Hadar (Ethiopia), and at Olduvai Gorge (Tanzania). According to Cooke, the dating at Lake Turkana (formerly Lake Rudolf) was too high by about 800,000 years. The pigs at Turkana told him so.[222]

From looking at the R.A.T.E measurements at Grand Canyon and the wild swings re KNM-ER 1470 (212-230 Ma to 1.88Ma) one can only conclude that radioisotope 'dates' are anything but. Even when different methods come to the same conclusion, if the evolutionary expectations are not met, then the 'dates' can be discarded in favour of more acceptable ones. Detecting the ratio of parent isotope to daughter isotope is a brilliant piece of scientific skill. To conclude that said ratio is tantamount to assessing age is, however, unwarranted.

Still, one is left with the question as to why the 'daughter' elements are so high in relation to the 'parent' elements. Two observations can be made.

As mentioned in the case of helium retention in zircon crystals, there was a phase or two of accelerated nuclear decay in earth history. The first was probably during creation week, particularly on day 3 when dry land appeared. God may have used the sudden burst of energy to provide sufficient heat to cause the vertical rise of the continental land mass. The second episode was probably at the initiation of the Flood and part of the mechanism to cause the break-up of the fountains of the great deep.

The second observation is that the heavier the parent isotope the more rapid the decay. Another way of looking at it is that the heavier atoms decayed by more *alpha* decay than lighter ones which utilize more

Introduction to How Old is Time?

beta decay. This observation would account for the different parent-daughter ratios of different elements.

A further evidence of accelerated nuclear decay is the presence of ^{238}U, ^{210}Po, ^{214}Po and ^{218}Po radiohalos in biotite flakes in granite. Biotite flakes are the small black flecks found throughout granite. Within the biotite are found the previously mentioned zircon crystals. The uranium that is in the zircons emits radiation into the surrounding biotite. As a result of physical deformities in the biotite (which consists of layers with intervening spaces), collection points are formed that trap the respective isotopes which were carried by hydrothermal fluids of the cooling granite. The uranium would collect in one spot producing the various poloniums[223] in others. As they decay their radiation discolours the biotite in the form of a sphere. When examined in cross-section they appear as concentric circles. The number of circles and intervening distances are determined by the isotope involved. A point to remember is that polonium isotopes are extremely short lived (ranging from half lives of 138.4 days for ^{210}Po, to 164 microseconds for ^{214}Po). ^{238}U on the other hand has a half life of 4.5 billion years.

The following schematic and description are by Andrew Snelling:

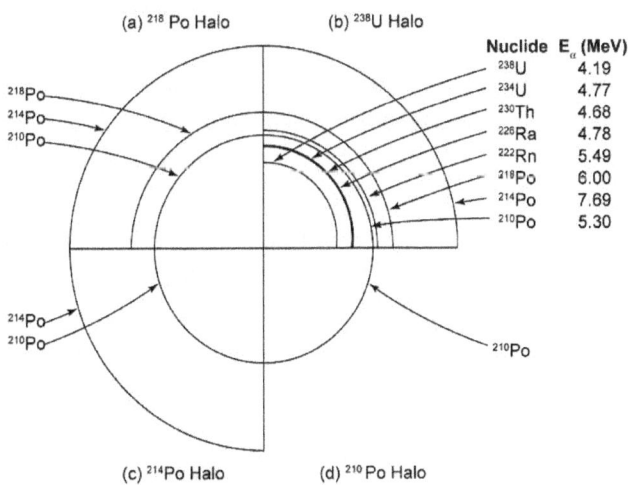

Composite schematic drawing of the radiation rings in (a) a polonium-218 radiohalo (three rings), (b) a uranium radiohalo (eight rings), (c) a polonium-214 radiohalo (two rings), and (d) a polonium-210 radiohalo (one ring). The different radiation energies (E) are listed.[224]

113

A major paper by Andrew Snelling *Radio Halos in Granites: Evidence for Accelerated Nuclear Decay*[225] is perhaps the most thorough treatment available. In the following abstract I have highlighted both the reference to accelerated decay and the reference to rapid cooling of the originally molten granite deposits (pluton - igneous underground rock formed from consolidation of magma). Both of these phenomena are contrary to evolutionary expectations.

The ubiquitous presence of ^{238}U and ^{210}Po, ^{214}Po, and ^{218}Po radiohalos in the same biotite flakes within granitic plutons formed during the Flood testifies to the simultaneous formation of these radiohalos. **Thus if the Po radiohalos were formed in just a few days while the fully-formed ^{238}U radiohalos were simultaneously generated by at least 100 million years worth (at today's rates) of radioactive decay, radioisotope decay had to have been accelerated.** Therefore, conventional radioisotope dating of rocks based on assuming constancy of decay rates is grossly in error. Accelerated radioisotope decay of ^{238}U in zircons within the biotites rapidly formed the ^{238}U radiohalos and produced large quantities of the short-lived ^{222}Rn and Po isotopes. Hydrothermal fluids released by the cooling granitic magmas then transported those isotopes along the biotites' cleavage planes to deposit the Po isotopes in chemically conducive, adjacent lattice defect sites, on average only 1 mm or less distant. The hydrothermal fluids progressively replenished the supply of Po isotopes to the deposition sites as the Po isotopes decayed to form the Po radiohalos. Because of the annealing of α-tracks above 150°C, all the radiohalos only formed below 150°C. However, the U-decay and hydrothermal fluid transport started while the granitic rocks were crystallizing at higher temperatures. **Therefore, the granitic magmas must have cooled rapidly or else the short-lived Po isotopes would have decayed before radiohalos could have formed. It is thus estimated that granitic plutons must have cooled within 6-10 days, and that the various Po radiohalos formed within**

hours to just a few days. The heat generated by accelerated radioisotope decay and tectonic processes during the Flood would have annealed all radiohalos in Precambrian (pre-Flood) granitic rocks at that time, so the few radiohalos now observed in these granitic rocks had to have formed subsequently by secondary hydrothermal fluid transport of ^{222}Rn and Po isotopes in their biotites during the Flood. While convective flows of hydrothermal fluids moved and dissipated heat from granitic plutons in days, that mechanism alone would not seem capable of removing the enormous quantities of heat generated by accelerated radioisotope decay over that brief timescale. Other mechanisms must have operated to allow for the survival of the biotites and their ^{238}U and Po radiohalos. The discovery of plentiful Po radiohalos in metamorphic rocks extends the application of the hydrothermal fluid transport model for Po radiohalo formation to these rocks. This means that hydrothermal fluids transformed deeply-buried sedimentary rocks to regional metamorphic complexes, which then had to have cooled within days for the Po radiohalos to have formed. Additionally, the prolific Po radiohalos in granitic and metamorphic rocks and veins that host metallic ore lodes reflect the passage of the hydrothermal fluids that transported and deposited the metallic ores. This suggests such hydrothermal ore veins formed rapidly, and that Po radiohalos could provide an exploration tool for locating new ore lodes. Thus Po radiohalos provide powerful evidence of many rapid geological processes consistent with both the year-long catastrophic global Biblical Flood, and a young earth. (emphasis mine)

To repeat, note two things: accelerated nuclear decay occurred and so did rapid cooling of granitic bodies. Snelling refers to cooling methods other than convection being responsible for the removal of the excessive heat generated by the accelerated decay. We consider now what a possible (probable) mechanism may have been.

I. Where Did the Heat Go?

Such decay would cause a massive radiation of heat from the mantle - sufficient to melt the crust. Since the crust didn't melt during, say, the Flood, we can ask "Where did the heat go?"

A possible answer is to be found in the expansion of the fabric of space. Seventeen times the Old Testament refers to God "stretching out," "spreading out" the heavens. If this act of spatial expansion was initiated in the creation week and given further impetus during the Flood then there are cosmological implications involved (see later). There would also be consequences for heat removal.

As D. Russell Humphreys states:[226]

> There is a well-understood but poorly publicized mechanism in general relativity that accounts for the loss [of heat]. The result of calculations using that mechanism is [Robertson and Noonan 1968, p.356]: 'Therefore, the radiation energy which is lost in an expanding universe is used up as work in aiding the expansion.

This possibility is consistent with the witness of Scripture and with the carefully worked out mathematics of General Relativity. The expansion of the fabric of space is the widely given explanation for red shifts of galaxies and stars. Red shifts are now seen as cosmological and not Doppler in nature. This will be dealt with below. The suggestion of Humphreys re the expansion of space holds considerable promise and creation scientists are studying this issue. The fact remains that radiohalos indicate both accelerated nuclear decay and rapid cooling of granitic plutons.

J. The Moon's Recession from the Earth

We come to an easily verifiable method of seeing relative youthfulness, namely a theoretical and observational phenomenon. The theoretical is the law of conservation of angular momentum. The observable phenomena are NASA laser based measurements which accurately records the recession rate of the moon.

In the case of the earth-moon system the conservation of angular momentum simply means that the sum of the rotational momentum of

Introduction to How Old is Time?

the earth and the orbital momentum of the moon must remain constant so that the total momentum is conserved.

The earth's rotation, however, is slowing down due to tidal friction. As the moon's gravitational force causes the oceans to 'bulge' and consequently to impact the continental margins as tides, the earth slows down at a rate of 0.002 seconds per century.[227] This represents a decrease in angular momentum on the part of the earth. In order to keep the earth-moon momentum conserved the moon's angular momentum must increase by the corresponding amount. Thus the moon increases its velocity and recedes from the earth at a rate of approximately 4 centimetres a year. To cite the Lunar and Planetary Society's article on Apollo 14's laser reflector:

> The Laser Ranging Retroreflector experiment has produced many important measurements. These include an improved knowledge of the Moon's orbit and the rate at which the Moon is receding from Earth (currently 3.8 centimeters per year) and of variations in the rotation of the Moon. These variations in rotation are related to the distribution of mass inside the Moon and imply the existence of a small core, with a radius of less than 350 kilometers, somewhat smaller than the limits imposed by the passive seismic and magnetometer experiments. These measurements have also improved our knowledge of changes of the Earth's rotation rate and the precession of its spin axis and have been used to test Einstein's theory of relativity.[228]

Given both the theoretical and empirically measured rate of lunar recession from the earth, this immediately brings up the issue of time constraints. As we go back in time the moon would be closer to the earth. If the earth-moon system were created 6000 years ago, then it would now be less than a kilometre further out than it was at its creation - hardly noticeable to the naked eye (in fact, probably not noticeable at all).

If, on the other hand, the earth-moon system is 4.5 billion years old then the problems are insuperable. 'Just' 1.3 billion years ago the moon would have been at the earth's Roche limit. This is the distance from a planet (in this case the earth) in which the moon would be ripped apart by differential terrestrial gravity. In this particular case the distance is 1.84×10^7 m. This represents approximately 5% of the moon's current distance. Furthermore, if it had left the Roche limit 4.5 billion years ago it would now be 20% further out - which it clearly is not.

Some evolutionists have invoked the possibility of lower tides in the far past. This runs into the simple fact that if the moon were appreciably closer to the earth the tides would be much greater and the transfer of angular momentum correspondingly so. Some have posited that the earth was configured differently with a massive polar continent and an equatorial continent with an unimpeded ocean.[229] Thus the tides would not be exercising friction against north-south continental shorelines. Such a continental distribution has no geophysical support and is, therefore, a somewhat forced attempt to preserve billions of years. Indeed, many lunar scientists have recognized the impossibility of satisfactorily explaining a self forming moon 4.5 billion years old.

Lunar scientist Irwin Shapiro used to joke that 'the best explanation [of lunar formation conundrums] was observational error—the moon does not exist'. The situation has not fundamentally changed, for lunar scientist Jack Lissauer recalled this anecdote as continuing to apply in a post-impact theory paper.[230]

The abstract of Lissauer's *Nature* paper states:
Theory has it that the Moon grew within a disk of material splashed out of the Earth by a body the size of Mars. According to new calculations, however, the impacting body was at least twice that size.[231]

What this in effect means is that the popular impact model for lunar formation faces enormous difficulties leading to the humorous observation cited above.

In conclusion, a moon created by God about six thousand years ago fits perfectly well with what we know of science. The 4.5 billion year

Introduction to How Old is Time?

old earth-moon system is an article of faith in defiance of known laws of physics.

K. THE EARLY FAINT SUN PROBLEM

This is an issue first noted by Carl Sagan and George Mullen in 1972.[232] The sun is believed to be 4.6 billion years old. Its heat is generated by nuclear fusion with hydrogen atoms fusing into helium thus releasing heat. The problem is that four billion years ago the Sun's energy output would only be 70%-75% of today's rate. Consequently, global temperature would have been below the freezing point of seawater and the planet would have been icebound (given current greenhouse gas and albedo conditions).

The earliest fossil record indicates, however, that the earth had a warm climate with an abundance of liquid water. Thus the problem is apparent.

There are logically only two major ways to solve this problem if in fact the earth is 4.6 billion years old.

Greenhouse atmospheric conditions were such that they trapped incoming heat much more than they do today. Originally CO_2 was seen as the primary agent but more recently, researchers, after analysing the 'haze' surrounding Titan, Saturn's largest moon, propose methane, nitrogen and ammonia:

> The University of Colorado at Boulder scientists believe the haze was made up primarily of methane and nitrogen chemical byproducts created by reactions with light, said CU-Boulder doctoral student Eric Wolf, lead study author. Not only would the haze have shielded early Earth from UV light, it would have allowed gases like ammonia to build up, causing greenhouse warming and perhaps helped to prevent the planet from freezing over.[233]

This would, however, require a delicate balancing act, since as the Sun was gradually approaching today's thermal output, the atmosphere would have to correspondingly be losing its greenhouse abilities. If not, the earth would become a boiling cauldron.

Secondly, the earth's albedo was greatly diminished. This could be accomplished by a worldwide ocean with just a few small land surfaces. The ocean would provide a global heat absorber since it is darker than land and this would in turn warm the planet sufficiently for life to develop and flourish. Rosing *et al* state in their *Nature* abstract that:

> Our model calculations suggest that the lower albedo of the early Earth provided environmental conditions above the freezing point of water, thus alleviating the need for extreme greenhouse-gas concentrations to satisfy the faint early Sun paradox.[234]

Again, this would require a delicate balancing mechanism since as the Sun's thermal output was increasing, the reflective ability of the earth would have to be correspondingly increasing (increasing land surface, cloud cover) or once again the issue of runaway warming would ensue.

The more one considers the various scenarios proposed, the more one is tempted to opt for Occam's razor - the simplest solution with the most consistent explanatory power is the most likely.[235] The earth and sun were created 6000 years ago and they were both fully mature and functional. There was never a 'faint sun paradox' and all attempts to 'solve' it are dealing with a problem that never existed.

L. The Jovian Planets[236]

The Jovian planets (Saturn, Jupiter, Uranus and Neptune) have characteristics that are far more consistent with a young solar system than a 4.5 billion year time frame. We have already seen the creationist prediction by D. Russell Humphreys on the magnetic fields of Uranus and Neptune and that the creationist position fit the data and that the evolutionary position did not. I will now consider some other characteristics of all four gas giants.

The first feature is that they all radiate more heat than they receive from the sun. Jupiter radiates 3.0×10^{17} watts, mostly in the infrared, which is twice the amount it receives from the sun.[237] Saturn produces half the irradiative energy of Jupiter but since it is only thirty percent

Introduction to How Old is Time?

the mass of the larger planet, it is actually producing twice the power per unit mass. Uranus and Neptune likewise emit energy in excess of that received from the sun though not as much as the two giant planets. Thus all four have internal energy sources.

The standard explanation for this is gravitational contraction causing energy to be released as heat. According to the virial theorem which states that, for a stable, self-gravitating, spherical distribution of equal mass objects (stars, galaxies, etc.), the total kinetic energy of the objects is equal to minus 1/2 times the total gravitational potential energy. In other words, the potential energy must equal the kinetic energy, within a factor of two.[238]

This means that in the case of gravitational contraction half of the energy is radiated out of the planet as heat and the other half is absorbed as internal energy.[239]

The physical models derived from the virial theorem indicate that the energy required for the contraction process to function would need Jupiter to be 600 million years older than the solar system which is purported to be 4.5 billion years old.[240]

In order to explain how this heat could be generated without relying solely upon gravitational contraction two main approaches have been put forward.

The first was to posit that helium was being separated out of the liquid hydrogen mantle due to it being heavier and that gravity was causing it to fall towards the core.[241] This would cause the planet to oscillate as well as produce heat. However, it has become apparent from further research that at the most, only 30% of the helium mass could be at the core.[242] This would be far too little to cause the heat radiation which has been measured.

The second approach has been to propose nuclear fusion to be operating in the planet's interior.[243] This would involve deuterium-deuterium (D-D) fusion occurring in the interior of Jupiter. Deuterium is a heavier version of ordinary hydrogen having a nucleus of one proton and one neutron.[244] In order for D-D fusion to take place it requires a temperature greater than that of the solar interior. [The Sun's mass and consequent gravitational compression help push the D atoms to fuse with one another.] However, standard models of a 4.5 billion year old Jupiter posit a temperature of far too low to accommodate the claimed D-D reaction.[245] The only way a temperature capable of generating D-D fusion could be achieved would be the infall of gases in a recently formed Jupiter (Samec). Furthermore, the deuterium would have to be in just the right place at just the right time. Ouyed *et al* posit that the deuterium quickly separated out from the normal hydrogen mantle and formed a cover around the core before the planet began to cool. It then ignited and the fusion process continues to this day. They speculate that if all the deuterium settled around the core it could continue to burn for a hundred billion years. In effect, Jupiter becomes a star. The same process would have to happen with Saturn, Uranus and Neptune since they all emit excessive thermal energy. The probability of all four gas giants having the same fortuitous timing and sequence of formation strains credulity, particularly since they do not all have the same chemical composition or mass.

Ouyed *et al* admit their model is debatable since they recognize the rather serious concerns their proposal raises. In light of the difficulty, indeed for practical purposes, impossibility of explaining how after 4.5 billion years the Jovian planets could still be emitting heat, Samec writes:

> So how do we explain the excess energy given off by the jovian planets? When God created these planets, the total energy they contained was the sum of the work He supplied plus any gravitational potential energy. The total energy of these processes was converted into heat and this is the source of the primordial energy. Uniformitarians postulate that the primordial energy was derived from accretion in the solar nebulae. Both models give the same result—the jovian planets were initially hot. It is only because the uniformitarian assumes the planets are billions of years old that he runs into problems.
>
> However, once we accept that *the jovian planets are young*, the excess energy problem disappears. There is no need of a solution. Since the jovian planets have only recently been formed, they do not need nuclear processes to keep them hot for non-

Introduction to How Old is Time?

existent evolutionary aeons. Rather, they are only thousands of years old and have been hot since they were created.

This is clearly the most reasonable of the proffered explanations for the thermal radiation of the four gas giants.

M. GALAXIES WIND UP TOO FAST
This argument is quite simple to understand and is again recognized as a significant issue that needs to be solved. Essentially the argument is that since spiral galaxies have interior zones that rotate faster than the outer zones, they could not retain their spiral shape for more than 100 million years before becoming featureless disks. The evolutionary problem is that the galaxies are supposed to be at least 10 billion years old. Yet for all appearances they must be less than 100 million years old. In fact, from appearance they could be just a few thousand years old.

There have been different attempts to get around this problem. D. Russell Humphreys explains:

Evolutionists call this 'the winding-up dilemma', which they have known about for fifty years. They have devised many theories to try to explain it, each one failing after a brief period of popularity. The same 'winding-up' dilemma also applies to other galaxies.

For the last few decades the favored attempt to resolve the dilemma has been a complex theory called 'density waves'.[1] The theory has conceptual problems, has to be arbitrarily and very finely tuned, and lately has been called into serious question by the Hubble Space Telescope's discovery of very detailed spiral structure in the central hub of the 'Whirlpool' galaxy, M51. [2 247]

http://hubblesite.org/newscenter/archive/releases/2005/12/image/a

The Galaxy's name M51a/b signifies item no. 51 in Charles Messier's astronomical catalogue. Messier was the astronomer who first discovered it in 1773. The letter 'a' refers to the larger galaxy while 'b' refers to the smaller companion galaxy. It is also referred to as NGC 5194/5 (New General Catalogue of Nebulae and Clusters of Stars, catalogue # 5194/5).

The fact that these attempts are made is eloquent testimony that for spiral galaxies the age issue is a huge problem for evolutionists and that those who are specialists in the field know it.

N. Population Growth

World population and the demographics of Israel as a control:

(1) According to the Bible, all human beings on the earth today are descended from Noah, his wife and their three sons (Shem, Ham and Japheth) and their three wives (8 people in all). As to be expected, all people were of "...one language and a common speech..." (Genesis 11:1). Furthermore, it was at the tower of Babel (perhaps the fifth generation from the flood - cf. Genesis 10:25 & 11:17, 18) that God, as an act of judgment, divided the human race into the various language groups. It would appear from Genesis 10:1-32 that this original division was into approximately 16 ancestral groups. In Genesis 10:32 we read the summary formula, "These are the clans of Noah's sons, according to

their lines of descent (Heb. *toledoth*), within their nations (Heb. *goyim*). From these the nations (Heb. *goyim*) spread out after the flood."

(2) Current World Population: there are approximately 7 billion people divided into nearly 12,000 "ethno-linguistic" groups speaking around 6,500 languages (these figures are open to challenge but they are, nevertheless, a good indicator of where we are today).[248]

(3) Is it realistic to get from (1) to (2) within the time frame provided in the Bible (i.e., within approximately 4500 years)?

The answer to (3) is yes. In fact, the argument from population growth is one of the simplest and most obvious supports for the Genesis account.

Illustration:[249] $P_n = 2(cn-x+1)(cx-1)â(c-1)$

This equation gives the world population n generations after the first family, for an average life-span of x generations and an average number of children growing to maturity and marriage of 2c per family. The equation clearly demonstrates how rapidly populations can grow under favorable conditions.

Example: in Genesis, the Flood would be placed at ca. 2400 B.C. The equation then would be:

$4{,}600{,}000{,}000 = 2(c)^{100}$
$c = (2{,}300{,}000{,}000)^{.01} = 1.24$ (or approx. 1.25)

Thus the average family must have had 2.5 children in order to bring the population to its 1984 magnitude in 100 generations (assuming a generation = 43 yrs.)

Since the world's population in 2012 is ca. 7 billion and, since as Morris states, he is using an ultra-conservative generation figure of 43 years whereas something around 25 would be more accurate (on a global scale) one can easily ask "Why is the population so low starting with eight people 4400 years ago?"

Kitcher's evolutionary response to the above:

Re. Morris' calculations: "It should be fairly obvious that this is a blunder. There is every reason to believe that the rate of growth of the human population has not been constant, but has fluctuated quite wildly in the past. Indeed, it is surely an oversimplification to consider the growth of the human population except during the last few centuries. If we think about the distribution of humans at the dawn of recorded history, then it is far more realistic to conceive the human race as consisting of a number of relatively small populations. Some of these were fairly successful and were able to expand until they reached the maximum size their local environments could bear. Others were wiped out by disease, dwindling resources, or competition with other groups. The entire human race may be regarded as a single population only for the most recent past; that is, it has only been very recently that humans have had the power, though not necessarily the desire, to redistribute the earth's resources so as to overcome local limits imposed by the local environment.[250]

Creationist response to the preceding argument: Though Kitcher argues for a wildly fluctuating world population, there would still be an aggregate number of people on the globe at any given time. The question is "how many on average?" With the kind of time frame that evolution calls for there are real difficulties. Note the following from Morris, *Biblical Basis,* 424, 425:

Totals Since the Beginning: "Although it is not possible to determine accurate totals, it is of interest to try to estimate how many people have been born since the beginning.... The evolutionist may object and say that the rate has drastically accelerated only in recent centuries. So let us consider that the 'normal' growth was such as to produce only the earth's population as it was at the time of Christ, about 200,000,000 people. This is the oldest date for which anyone has even a reasonable guess as to the population. The value of C necessary to give 200,000,000 people in 25,000 generations (number of 40-year generations in 1 million years of human existence) can be calculated as 1.0007 (i.e., 2.0014 children per couple) and the corresponding number of people who had lived and died in that period would still be over 300 billion. Therefore, using the most conservative figures for which we have even the remotest

Introduction to How Old is Time?

justification, if the theory of human evolution is true, there must have been at least 300 billion people who lived and died on the earth...." by the time of Christ's coming. Where are the bodies?

D. Russell Humphreys observes:
Evolutionary anthropologists say that the Stone Age lasted for at least 100,000 years, during which time the world population of Neanderthal and Cro-magnon men was roughly constant, between 1 and 10 million. All that time they were burying their dead with artefacts. By this scenario, they would have buried at least four billion bodies. If the evolutionary time scale is correct, buried bones should be able to last much longer than 100,000 years. So many of the supposed four billion Stone Age skeletons should still be around (and certainly the buried artefacts). Yet only a tiny fraction of this number has been found. This implies the Stone Age was much shorter than evolutionists think, a few hundred years in many areas.[251]

Note that Humphreys is giving a minimal set of numbers.
Israel as a Control:
Consider the nation Israel, which began with the patriarch Jacob about 3,700 years ago. Despite tremendous persecutions over the centuries, and despite the lack of a national homeland for much of their history, the people of Israel have maintained their national identity and now number probably about 14 million people. This population could have been produced in 3,700 years if we assume the average family size was only 2.4 children (instead of 2.5, to allow for the losses due to the above-mentioned factors), but still assuming a life-span of one 43-year generation. Using these figures, the formula yields a present world population of 13,900,000 Israelites. (These assumptions are obviously far too conservative for the first several generations of Israelites at least, for Jacob had twelve sons, and his descendants numbered probably over two million by the time of the exodus from Egypt (Num.1:45-47).[252]

Steven Robinson comments in the course of dealing with ancient Egyptian population growth on the general topic of technology and civilization:

> The terms Stone Age, Bronze Age and Iron Age can therefore be misleading. Bronze does not replace stone on a large scale until several centuries into the Bronze Age - in the second millennium - and long after the rise of the earliest civilizations. These civilizations rose while the use of stone was still common and they developed metallurgy as a consequence of their growth - the growth, not least, of their populations. The development of metallurgy was not, therefore the prime-mover of historical development, and the history of man prior to the rise of civilization was not determined by a failure to develop metallurgy; stone technology exercised no retarding influence. The idea that civilization rose suddenly out of a darkness to which hundreds of thousands of years must be attributed has no basis. Rather, there was a continuum, and the pace of change during the historical period was short.[253]

The evidence from population growth is far more favourable to the Biblical time frame than the evolutionary one. Conversely, it represents a major problem for evolution.

Why? Because if the human race is a million years old (or even a hundred thousand), the world's population would be impossibly large and the number of bodily remains would be in the multiple billions. On the other hand, everything we know about the mathematics of population growth indicates that starting with a single family 4400 years ago (Noah and his wife, their three sons and their three wives) there is more than enough time to arrive at the current population.

O. Distant Starlight

For many people the issue of distant star light is a major stumbling block to believing in a young universe. What many do not realise, however, is that the evolutionary 'Big Bang' has just as much of a problem with light travel and age of the cosmos. It also has major problems with star

Introduction to How Old is Time?

and galaxy formation and this is recognized by prominent specialists who themselves believe in Big Bang cosmology. We will consider both of these issues before considering creationist cosmological theories.

Astrophysicist Dr. Jason Lisle explains the background to the light travel time problem:

> In 1964/5, Penzias and Wilson discovered that the earth was bathed in a faint microwave radiation, apparently coming from the most distant observable regions of the universe, and this earned them the Nobel Prize for Physics in 1978.[1] This Cosmic Microwave Background (CMB) comes from all directions in space and has a characteristic temperature.[2] [3] While the discovery of the CMB has been called a successful prediction of the big bang model,[4] it is actually a *problem* for the big bang. This is because the temperature of the CMB creates a light-travel–time problem for big bang models of the origin of the universe.[254]

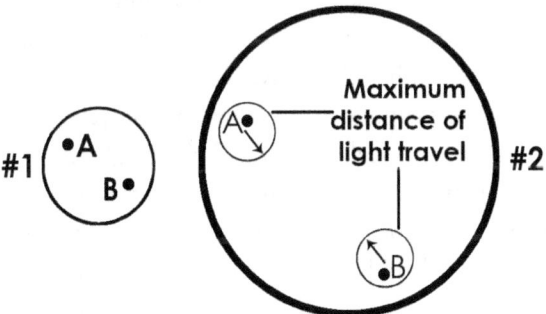

(1) According to Big Bang Theory, points A and B start out at different temperatures.

(2) Today, A and B have still not had enough time to exchange light, but are the same temperature.

The above explanation by Jason Lisle explains the 'horizon' problem or the 'light travel' problem. He sums up the situation as follows:

The big bang requires that opposite regions of the visible universe must have exchanged energy by radiation, since these regions of space look the same in CMB maps. But there has not been enough time for light to travel this distance. Both biblical creationists and big bang supporters have proposed a variety of possible solutions to light-travel–time difficulties in their respective models. So big-bangers should not criticize creationists for hypothesizing potential solutions, since they do the same thing with their own model. The horizon problem remains a serious difficulty for big bang supporters, as evidenced by their many competing conjectures that attempt to solve it. Therefore, it is inconsistent for supporters of the big bang model to use light-travel time as an argument against biblical creation, since their own notion has an equivalent problem.[255]

Before we will consider the evolutionary attempts to overcome the Big Bang's light travel time problem we will consider the issue of star and galaxy formation. I believe this is important since many media and, indeed, academic presentations of cosmology do not refer to this issue and people are left with the mistaken impression that the Big Bang has been 'proven' and that all astronomers see it as having explanatory power far greater than any other alternative. Many people believe that since it posits a beginning (as opposed to an eternal universe) it fits in with a creationist position. Though theoretically at first glance, this would seem to be the case, many practitioners tend toward the atheistic position.

Regarding its lack of explanatory power two quotes from prominent researchers who accept Big Bang cosmology are quite illuminating. The first is Dr. James Trefil, Robinson Professor of Physics, George Mason Univ. Va. who was named chair of the Gemant Award Selection Committee of the American Institute of Physics. He states:

There shouldn't be galaxies out there at all, and even if there are galaxies, they shouldn't be grouped together the way they are....

The problem of explaining the existence of galaxies has proved to be one of the thorniest in cosmology. By all rights,

Introduction to How Old is Time?

they just shouldn't be there, yet there they sit. It's hard to convey the depth of the frustration that this simple fact induces among scientists.[256]

The other quote is from Stephen Hawking (emphasis mine):

> This picture of the universe (Big Bang)...is in agreement with all the observational evidence that we have today. Nevertheless, it leaves a **number of important questions unanswered:**... Despite the fact that the universe is so uniform and homogeneous on a large scale it contains local irregularities, such as **stars and galaxies.** These are thought to have developed from small differences in the density of the early universe from one region to another. What was the origin of these density fluctuations?[257]

Both of these quotations are representative of something well known to the experts but generally unknown to others. Why is the problem of star (and galaxy) formation so difficult to solve? Werner Gitt sums up the reason:

> Evolutionists generally believe that stars formed by the collapse of gas clouds under gravity. This is supposed to generate the millions of degrees required for nuclear fusion.
>
> But most clouds would be so hot that outward pressure would prevent collapse. Evolutionists must find a way for the cloud to cool down. One such mechanism might be through molecules in the cloud colliding and radiating enough of the heat away.
>
> But according to theory, the 'big bang' made mainly hydrogen, with a little helium—the other elements supposedly formed inside stars. Helium can't form molecules at all, so the only molecule that could be formed would be molecular hydrogen (H_2). Even this is easily destroyed by ultraviolet light, and usually needs dust grains to form—and dust grains require heavier elements. So the only coolant left is atomic hydrogen, and this would leave gas clouds over a hundred times too hot to collapse.

Abraham Loeb of Harvard's Center for Astrophysics says: 'The truth is that we don't understand star formation at a fundamental level.[1][258]

Having seen the insuperable difficulties connected with star formation I now draw attention to the Big Bang's light-travel-time problem and evolutionary attempts to solve it. Once again we turn to Jason Lisle. I include his eleven references in the main body of this document:

> However, the inflation scenario is far from certain. There are many different inflation models, each with its set of difficulties. Moreover, there is no consensus on which (if any) inflation model is correct. A physical mechanism that could cause the inflation is not known, though there are many speculations. There are also difficulties on how to turn off the inflation once it starts—the 'graceful exit' problem.[2] Many inflation models are known to be wrong—making predictions that are not consistent with observations,[3] such as Guth's original model.[4] Also, many aspects of inflation models are currently unable to be tested.
>
> Some astronomers do not accept inflationary models and have proposed other possible solutions to the horizon problem. These include: scenarios in which the gravitational constant varies with time,[5] the 'ekpyrotic model' which involves a cyclic universe,[6] scenarios in which light takes 'shortcuts' through extra (hypothetical) dimensions,[7] 'null-singularity' models,[8] and models in which the speed of light was much greater in the past.[9,10] (Creationists have also pointed out that a changing speed of light may solve light-travel–time difficulties for biblical creation.[11])
>
> In light of this disagreement, it is safe to say that the horizon problem has not been decisively solved.

Lisle's References and notes:
1) This notion does not violate relativity, which merely prevents objects travelling faster than c *through* space, whereas in the

inflation proposal it is space *itself* that expands and carries the objects with it.

2) Kraniotis, G.V., String cosmology, *International Journal of Modern Physics A* **15**(12):1707–1756, 2000.

3) Wang, Y., Spergel, D. and Strauss, M., Cosmology in the next millennium: Combining microwave anisotropy probe and Sloan digital sky survey data to constrain inflationary models, *The Astrophysical Journal* **510**:20–31, 1999.

4) Coles, P. and Lucchin, F., *Cosmology: The Origin and Evolution of Cosmic Structure*, John Wiley & Sons Ltd, Chichester, p. 151, 1996.

5) Levin, J. and Freese, K., Possible solution to the horizon problem: Modified aging in massless scalar theories of gravity, *Physical Review D (Particles, Fields, Gravitation, and Cosmology)* **47**(10):4282–4291, 1993.

6) Steinhardt, P. and Turok, N., A cyclic model of the universe, *Science* **296**(5572):1436–1439, 2002.

7) Chung, D. and Freese, K., Can geodesics in extra dimensions solve the cosmological horizon problem? *Physical Review D (Particles, Fields, Gravitation, and Cosmology)* **62**(6):063513-1–063513-7, 2000.

8) Célérier, M. and Szekeres, P., Timelike and null focusing singularities in spherical symmetry: A solution to the cosmological horizon problem and a challenge to the cosmic censorship hypothesis, *Physical Review D* **65**:123516-1–123516-9, 2002.

9) Albrecht, A. and Magueijo, J., Time varying speed of light as a solution to cosmological puzzles, *Physical Review D (Particles, Fields, Gravitation, and Cosmology)* **59**(4):043516-1–043516-13, 1999.

10) Clayton, M. and Moffat, J., Dynamical mechanism for varying light velocity as a solution to cosmological problems, *Physics Letters B* **460**(3–4):263–270, 1999.

11) For a summary of the c-decay implications, see: Wieland, C., Speed of light slowing down after all? Famous physicist makes headlines, *TJ* **16**(3):7–10, 2002.

Having seen that distant starlight and indeed the very formation of stars and galaxies present real problems to evolutionary astronomers it is now time to consider creationist approaches to the issue. First we will consider some Biblical data. It was noted above that there are in the Old Testament seventeen references to God 'stretching, spreading' out the heavens. Some refer to 'rolling up' the heavens. We will give these texts and then consider their implications as given by D. Russell Humphreys – an outstanding nuclear physicist who is also conversant in Biblical Hebrew. The texts are as follows:

"Who alone stretches out the heavens" - Job 9:8
"Stretching out heaven like a tent curtain" - Psalm 104:2
"Who stretches out the heavens like a curtain, and spreads them out like a tent to dwell in" – Isaiah 40:22
"He has stretched out the heavens" - Jeremiah 10:12
"The LORD who stretches the heavens" - Zechariah 12:1

There are at least 11 other similar verses in the Old Testament: 2 Sam. 22:10, Job 26:7, Job 37:18, Psalm 18:9, Psalm 144:5, Isaiah 42:5, Isaiah 44:24, Isaiah 45:12, Isaiah 48:13, Isaiah 51:13, and Jer. 51:15.

We will now consider Humphreys' observations taken from his book *Starlight and Time*.[259] Then we will note some caveats regarding his reading of these texts.

Generally we think of space as a vacuum, an empty volume. But how can a nothingness be stretched out as if it were a *something*, like a tent curtain? To get a clue, notice how scripture speaks of other things happening to the heavens. The heavens can be *torn* (Isaiah 64:1), *worn out like a garment* (Psalm 102:26), *shaken* (Hebrews 12:26, Haggai 2:6, Isaiah 13:13), *burnt up* (2 Peter 3:12), *split apart, (receded)* like a scroll when it is rolled up (Revelation 6:14), and *rolled up* like a mantle (Hebrews 1:12) or a scroll (Isaiah 34:4). It certainly sounds like space itself is a material of some sort!

"Interestingly enough, there are many phenomena in modern physics which point to such a concept (such as

Maxwell's displacement current and vacuum polarization), and physics even offers an explanation of why we cannot perceive this medium through which would be moving (Dirac's electron "sea" and Pauli's exclusion principle). The physics clues suggest that such a medium would be like an elastic solid. This might explain why the word *raqia* (Hebrew word translated by "firmament" or "expanse" in Genesis 1) ....(seems) to have some connection with solidity and firmness.

When He made firm the skies above - Proverbs 8:28

Can you, with Him, spread out the skies, strong as a molten mirror? - Job 37:18

Notice the reference to "rolling up" the heavens like a mantle or a scroll (Hebrews 1:12 and Isaiah 34:4). This suggests that (1) there is some dimension in which space is thin, (2) space can be bent, and (3) there exists a direction it can be bent toward. Thus these verses could be hinting that a fourth spatial dimension exists, even though we can't perceive it. (Time would be a fifth dimension, dealt with separately.) Again, this idea is not foreign to modern physics.

So if space is a material, some kind of "stuff" and not a nothingness, then it can be stretched out like a tent curtain, etc. This corresponds exactly to the picture behind the general relativistic expansion of the cosmos, where it is space itself which is being stretched out.

It can be claimed that the language of "stretching" does not justify reading relativistic cosmology -with its expansion of space- into the texts. The phrase may simply refer to God making a really big universe.[260] However, the language of 'rolling up' and 'strong as a molten mirror' seem to suggest concepts amenable to that kind of cosmology without being egregiously eisegetical (reading modern concepts into the text). There is always the issue of equivocal speech which may or may not imply a particular state of affairs.

These features have direct implications for the issue of distant starlight reaching the earth two days after the stars' creation on Day 4 -

so that Adam and Eve could look up on the day of their creation on Day 6 and see the starry heavens.

It is helpful to consider two ways in which some have sought to deal with this issue prior to time dilation theory. After looking at these approaches and time dilation a fourth option will be considered - Jason Lisle's anisotropic synchrony convention (ASC).

The first was 'apparent age' - just as Adam and Eve were fully mature adults, just as trees were full grown along with animals, etc., on the day of their creation – so God created stars etc. with the light already reaching the earth. The problem with this is that star light is not a blank. It contains a record of events that occurred at its source and in its journey. If the light was 'instantaneous' the record would, by definition, be false-- hardly a testimony to the glory of God.

The second approach is that the speed of light was millions of times faster than today's approximately 300,000 km./sec. In creationist circles it is identified with the work of Barry Setterfield and Trevor Norman. Actually, the decreasing speed of light was first proposed by M.E.J. Gheury de Bray in the official French astronomical journal in 1927 and later in 1934 (M.E.J. Gheury de Bray: "The Velocity of Light," *Nature*, 24 March 1934, p. 464ff.) Similarly, independent of Setterfield, Russian cosmologist V.S. Troitskii, at the Radio-physical Research Institute in Gorky is also postulating a rapidly decreasing speed of light (V.S. Troitskii: "Physical Constants and the Evolution of the Universe" *Astrophysics and Space Science*, Vol.139, No.2, December 1987, pp389-411.[261]

More recently, in 2003 a book by João Magueijo was published arguing that the variable speed of light can be used to solve the above mentioned horizon problem.[262] He is a leading physicist and lecturer at Imperial College, London with his Ph.D. from Cambridge. He was also a research fellow at the Royal Society for a few years. **I point this out to simply show that VSL has been invoked to rescue the Big Bang but when it is employed to solve distant starlight and Creation it is ridiculed.**

The major obstacle to VSL has been that a change in c[263] would involve a change in the 'fine structure constant' (symbol α) which was believed to be invariable. More recently it has been discovered that the 'constant' differs in light from distant stars than light from nearby stars. Admittedly, the VSL implied by this would be insufficient to accommodate the Genesis account or for that matter the horizon problem. Interestingly, Setterfield always argued that his VSL did not require a change in the fine structure constant.[264]

Nevertheless, as noted above, when variations of VSL are employed to solve the horizon problem it is seen as a possible solution. When applied to Genesis it is summarily discounted.

Having looked at decreasing speed of light I now look at the issue of time dilation which is the favoured approach of creation scientists today.

If Humphreys' understanding of the passages re 'stretching out the heavens' is correct then certain cosmological implications emerge. The expansion of space would have caused an enormous time-dilation event on the earth, meaning that Earth clocks would slow down by a trillion times compared to cosmic clocks. Time would flow in the cosmos at the same rate it does on earth now, but during the time-dilation period, Earth's clocks ran slow.

Even if one does not accept Humphreys' understanding of the Biblical citations, the time dilation approach would still be valid as a method of resolving the distant starlight issue. The minimal conclusion from Scripture is that God created the sun, moon and stars on the fourth day of creation. Furthermore, they were to be for 'signs and seasons' on the earth, i.e., they were visible. Third, they are numbered in the trillions. In Genesis 22:7 Abraham's descendants would be as numerous as "... the stars in the sky and as the sand on the seashore." This was God's way of saying they would greatly multiply. Though they would not number in the trillions, God is using a simile. The simile parallels the number of stars to the number of seashore sand grains. This immediately tells not only of a vast number but also of vast distances. This is because the number of stars visible to the naked eye in the clear night sky of the Middle East is under 10,000. Yet God says to Abraham that you cannot count them, for they are vast in number. Therefore, far from sight, they must extend massive distances. Finally, they are finite in number: Psalm 147:4 states "He determines the number of the stars and calls them each by name."

As a side note, the vast distances separating earth from the stars was well known in the classical and medieval world. Ptolemy's *Almagest* stated, "...the earth has sensibly the ratio of a point to its distance from the sphere of the so-called fixed stars...."[265] In other words, this corresponds to our contemporary understanding of the trillions of miles separating us from the stars outside our solar system. Since Ptolemy's *Amalgest* was the standard astronomy treatise in the medieval period we know this was also their understanding.

As far as the effect of space expansion upon time dilation, Dr. John Hartnett explains:

> The expansion of space caused an enormous time-dilation event on the earth, meaning that Earth clocks slowed by a trillion times compared to cosmic clocks. Time flowed in the cosmos at the same rate it does on earth now, but during the time-dilation period, Earth's clocks ran slow.
>
> During Creation Day 4 God created the heavenly bodies (stars and galaxies), and if Earth clocks ran slower by at least a few trillion times (an outcome that falls out of the new physics, as will be seen), then there would have been sufficient time (in a universe created some six thousand years ago by Earth clocks) for light to travel the vast distances of the universe.[266]

There are different ways of formulating this concept depending on the metric used. A metric is a method of measuring the distance between any two 'nearby' points in a space of two, three or more dimensions in terms of the coordinates of the two points. For instance we could measure the distance between Montreal and London, England, in one of three ways. By measuring a straight line on the surface of the globe (it would not actually be straight since the earth is curved). Or we could do a great circle route as the airlines do since that takes into account the sphericity of the planet and by so doing actually travel a shorter distance than the first option. We could also measure the distance envisaging an actual straight line passing through the earth from one city to the other. This would be the shortest measurement though no travel agent would suggest it. Each of these three methods can be called a metric. When

Introduction to How Old is Time?

dealing with space there are various metrics that can be used including incorporating velocity or acceleration of expansion into the metric as does Moshe Carmeli of Ben Gurion University, Israel. Hartnett uses Carmeli's metric in his cosmology.

The important thing for our purposes is that time is not absolute. Einstein argued that as you approach the speed of light time slows down. An astronaut travelling at such a speed would not be aware of anything different but when he returned to earth after he has recorded a few weeks of travel he would find that years or decades had passed on earth. That is a consequence of special relativity. General relativity, on the other hand deals with gravity. The closer one is to a center of gravity the slower time passes. For example, atomic clocks in Greenwich England (virtually at sea level) record five microseconds a year less than those in Boulder, Colorado (about a mile above sea level). Furthermore, atomic clocks have to be adjusted for GPS since time is progressing faster in the satellite than on earth - otherwise, there would be an error of a few hundred meters on your dashboard GPS.

Therefore, Hartnett's comments above are consistent with what we know of time's variability.

Another approach developed by Jason Lisle is to argue that the problem arises simply because of the time convention being used.[267] He calls for the use of anisotropic synchrony convention (ASC). Anisotropic is defined as "exhibiting properties with different values when measured in different directions." (Mirriam-Webster.com). This can be viewed as a phenomenological method of measuring the time of an event. Synchrony refers to events occurring 'simultaneously'. Convention refers to the fact that the definition of 'synchrony' is a matter of choice.

The speed of light is always determined by halving the two way speed. I.e., light is flashed from a source to a mirror and the time computed for the arrival of the return signal is then divided in half and in turn divided by distance. The one way speed of light cannot in itself be measured. This may seem of little importance but it has significant conceptual ramifications. Lisle comments:

> Einstein himself noted that attempts to measure the one-way speed of light are inherently circular. In discussing the

139

simultaneity of two bolts of lightning at A and B, as perceived by a person standing exactly in between them at M, he says,

...if only I knew that the light by means of which the observer at M perceives the lightning flashes travels along the length A → M with the same velocity as along the length B → M. But an examination would only be possible if we already had at our disposal the means of measuring time. It would thus appear as though we were moving here in a logical circle. (Einstein 1961, pp. 22–23).

Einstein rightly concludes that the one-way speed of light is not an empirical quantity of nature, but a choice of man. He states,

That light requires the same time to traverse the path A → M as for the path B → M is in reality neither a *supposition nor a hypothesis* about the physical nature of light, but a *stipulation* which I can make of my own freewill in order to arrive at a definition of simultaneity. (Einstein 1961, p. 23) [emphasis is in the original]

This conclusion is quite profound. Since we cannot (even in principle) ever measure the one-way speed of light, Einstein concludes that the one-way speed of light is not actually a property of nature, but a choice of man. Before Einstein, we might have assumed that the one-way speed of light (and thus, the corresponding synchrony convention) is a property of the universe—one that we are not clever enough to measure. But according to Einstein, the fact that we can never test a synchrony convention shows us something fundamental about the universe. Namely, it tells us that synchrony conventions are not a property of the universe, but are instead a system of measurement invented by man. According to the conventionality thesis, no experiment will ever be able to establish one synchrony convention over another, because synchronization systems are a human invention by which we measure other things—much like the metric system.[268]

In effect, synchrony is observer dependent. Lisle argues that ASC is the default biblical and indeed human convention. We speak of sunrise and sunset. Astronomers refer to a supernova as e.g., SN1987a (Supernova in 1987, first one observed that year). In these cases the terms are based on the observer's perception.

Lisle's position, though involving sophisticated math and 'light cones,' means that we consider the stars to have been made on the day their light became visible on earth, namely the fourth day. Since we do not know the one way speed of light we could easily say that to a hypothetical observer on earth (Adam would be created two days later) the light travel time could be said to be instantaneous.

If the ASC is used to generate a cosmology it necessarily follows that no matter where we look in the universe it will appear to be the same age, i.e., 6000 years. This is clearly a falsifiable prediction which can be confirmed or refuted. Lisle mentions a number of cosmic features such as blue stars, spiral galaxies, extra solar system planets with rings, which all look similar no matter how near or far they are. He argues that since the universe was created 'mature' that what appear to be two galaxies 'merging' may simply be the arrangement of matter that God created - not reflecting a history of any actual collision.

Thus far we have looked at four types of resolution to the distant starlight issue: apparent age, decreasing speed of light, time dilation and ASC. The first one seems inadequate, the second possible, though not endorsed by too many since there are serious physics problems apparently unresolved. The last two seem to have more going for them though from my reading, I find it difficult to choose.

I have a tendency to prefer the time dilation model because of some of the texts cited by Humphreys and also because of its (to my mind) aesthetic elegance. I would say, however, that both of them seem conceptually valid. In fact, Humphreys and Hartnett have different versions of the time dilation model since they employ different metrics and in turn each has refined or revised their initial work. Indeed, Hartnett now holds the evidence for expansion is equivocal though accepting time dilation. Humphreys has developed a metric which leads to a Euclidian timeless zone during creation week.[269] Hartnett likewise views the possibility of a currently static Euclidian universe as a possible reading of the evidence.[270] Who knows? There may yet be another approach to be developed. It was noted that the evolutionary Big Bang has the same issue to solve and thus its practitioners have no rationale to criticize creationist proposals.

Redemption -
The Hope Found In Jesus Christ

In my introduction I stated that my aim was to show that atheistic Darwinism is open to serious questioning and indeed falsified on several levels. I also argued that the Biblical account of origins is far more reasonable in light of modern science. I have argued that the standard evolutionary account of origins is really a faith commitment, indeed a religious commitment, in spite of the facts, in order to avoid any mention of the Creator. This is not to deny that many Christians try to combine the two accounts of world history. It is to say, however, that they are in a state of massive intellectual self contradiction.

I also stated that faith in Jesus Christ is the path to true hope. In the account of the Fall in Genesis 3:15, God speaks to the Serpent, who is identified with Satan, and gives the first prophecy of the coming Redeemer:

And I will put enmity
between you and the woman,
and between your seed and hers;
he will crush your head,
and you will strike his heel.

Note that the Redeemer is uniquely the Seed of the woman - ultimately fulfilled in the virgin birth of Christ. After the tower of Babel, God calls Abraham (a descendant of Shem) and promises him that through his seed all the nations of the world would be blessed. Later as Israel is formed from his descendants, prophets are raised up who give more detailed predictions about the coming of the Messiah. A crucial statement made by Isaiah 53:6;

> We all, like sheep, have gone astray,
> each of us has turned to our own way;
> and the LORD has laid on him
> the iniquity of us all.

This brings up the central core of our hope. The consequence of our rebellion against God is separation from Him. The result of our turning away from the Source of life is death. The Bible teaches that when Christ died on the cross, He, as the eternal Son of God, absorbed into Himself the consequences of our sin on the cross. His death was a substitution on our behalf. To demonstrate that He truly bore our sins and died in our place, He rose again from the dead on the third day. Forty days later He ascended into Heaven. This means that He forever remains the God-Man. After His ascension ten days later on the Jewish feast of *Shavuot* (also known by the Greek word *Pentecost*) He sent the Holy Spirit upon the early believers in Jerusalem. Today if anyone admits their need of Christ and turns away from their self centeredness and welcomes Him into their life He will come into them, granting them forgiveness of sin, the gift of the Holy Spirit and life everlasting.

The Bible tells us that Christ will return in power and glory and will judge the world. There will be a New Heaven and a New Earth with all effects of the Fall erased. This is an amazing hope if we put our trust in Christ, in His death for our sins and in His resurrection.

Jesus stated on different occasions that He would rise from the dead. One text among several is Matthew 17:22, 23:

> As they were gathering in Galilee, Jesus said to them, "The Son of Man is about to be delivered into the hands of men, and they will kill him, and he will be raised on the third day." And they were greatly distressed.

In John 2 Jesus is challenged by the religious leaders to give a sign of His authority:
> *So the Jews said to him, "What sign do you show us for doing these things?" Jesus answered them, "Destroy this temple, and in three days I will raise it up." The Jews then said, "It has taken forty-six years to build this temple, and will you raise it up in three days?" But he was speaking about the temple of his body. When therefore he was raised from the dead, his disciples remembered that he had said this, and they believed the Scripture and the word that Jesus had spoken.*

Jesus staked His claims to messiahship on His resurrection. The apostles likewise emphasized the resurrection of Christ. One example is Paul's statement in 1 Corinthians 15:14, 17-18:
> *And if Christ has not been raised, our preaching is useless and so is your faith.... And if Christ has not been raised, your faith is futile; you are still in your sins. Then those also who have fallen asleep in Christ are lost. If only for this life we have hope in Christ, we are of all people most to be pitied.*

Many think that trusting in Christ is simply a subjective decision unsupported by any evidence. As pointed out in the beginning of this book, the New Testament does not teach this. It tells us that
> *After his suffering, he presented himself to them and gave many convincing proofs that he was alive. He appeared to them over a period of forty days and spoke about the kingdom of God.* (Acts 1:3)

"Convincing proofs" is not exactly the language of subjectivity. Either He rose from the dead or He didn't. Paul was not adverse to giving evidence for Christ's resurrection. In 1 Corinthians 15:3-8 he gives a list of individuals who saw Christ after His resurrection.
> *For what I received I passed on to you as of first importance: that Christ died for our sins according to the Scriptures, that he was buried, that he was raised on the third day according to the*

> Scriptures, and that he appeared to Cephas [Peter] and then to the Twelve. After that, he appeared to more than five hundred of the brothers and sisters at the same time, most of whom are still living, though some have fallen asleep. Then he appeared to James, then to all the apostles, and last of all he appeared to me also, as to one abnormally born.

If there was no evidence for Christ's resurrection or if it was considered unnecessary to marshal the evidence then why would Paul spend ink on this topic?

> After all, it was Paul who told the Roman governor Festus that "What I am saying is true and reasonable." (Acts 26:25)

It was the apostle Peter who wrote:
> For we did not follow cleverly devised stories when we told you about the coming of our Lord Jesus Christ in power, but we were eyewitnesses of his majesty. He received honor and glory from God the Father when the voice came to him from the Majestic Glory, saying, "This is my Son, whom I love; with him I am well pleased." We ourselves heard this voice that came from heaven when we were with him on the sacred mountain.

The apostle emphasizes the personal eyewitness of himself and James and John to the transfiguration of Christ and states, because of this empirical evidence (among many others), the gospel was not "cleverly devised stories." Now, we do not live in the first century where we could interview these witnesses. But that is true of any historical event that occurred centuries before our time.

Nevertheless, we can, by using the normal canons of historical and legal argumentation, come to a conclusion as to whether or not Christ rose from the dead. Ultimately trusting Christ as Lord and Saviour is just that - trusting Him. That does not mean 'blind faith' as we have seen from the Bible itself. At this point I will show the historical case for the Lord's resurrection. In effect, this is the same kind of argument that would be used in a court room.

EVIDENCE FOR THE RESURRECTION

We know, not only from the Bible, but also from other early writings that Christianity spread far and wide throughout the 1st Century. This is so well known as to be beyond dispute.

Jesus was crucified when Pontius Pilate was governor of Judea. Not only the N.T. but Tacitus the Roman historian who despised Christianity makes reference to this in the late 1st century.

The tomb was guarded. A standard Roman guard unit consisted of sixteen crack troops with four on duty while twelve would be sleeping. A rota of four fresh troops after four hours would take their place. The ones resting would lie on the ground in front of the active guard unit. In Acts 12:4 we see Herod's guard unit (patterned after the Roman model) consisting of four squads of four soldiers each.

On the third day the tomb was empty and many claimed to have seen Him for a forty-day period at the end of which He ascended into heaven.

Possible explanations:

The disciples stole the body while the guards were sleeping and pretended He was alive.

Problem: No motive (they were defeated and discouraged). **No means** (Roman guard units were highly disciplined fighting units); and **no later recantations**: even though most died tortuous deaths.

Jesus only swooned on the cross and later revived in the tomb.

Problem: With this logic we would also assume that He somehow rolled aside a 2.5 ton stone and convinced people He was raised from the dead. However, the Romans knew how to kill a man and they made sure their victims were dead when they took them off the cross. Furthermore, the standard burial practices (body wrapped in cloth and spices) would probably suffocate a healthy person, let alone a severely wounded one.

The priests removed the body for safe keeping.

Problem: When Peter preached in Jerusalem on the day of Pentecost, all the priests had to do was to produce the body. They didn't, because they themselves didn't know where it was.

The women (Mary Magdalene, Joanna, et al.) went to the wrong tomb on Sunday morning.

Problem: to continue this thought, they looked into an empty tomb and falsely concluded that He had risen from the dead. Apparently also, the disciples, the soldiers and the priests all forgot where the tomb was (even though it belonged to a prominent Sanhedrin member, Joseph of Arimathea).

People only hallucinated about seeing the risen Christ.

Problem: the varied times of day, the different personalities involved, the different geographical locations and the fact that all the appearances stopped after the 40-day period make this virtually impossible. Furthermore, the body would still be in the tomb and the authorities could simply show it to the skeptical multitudes.

One explanation fits the evidence: Jesus Christ rose from the dead on the third day, showed Himself to be alive by many convincing proofs and then ascended into heaven. Ten days after the ascension the Holy Spirit descended on the day of Pentecost and the gospel began to spread throughout the world! Christ is risen! He is risen indeed! We can have eternal life through receiving Him into our hearts.

INTEGRITY OF SCRIPTURE

The New Testament has more manuscripts than any other document from the ancient world. In the manuscript comparison below, evidence is given about the date of composition, the date of the earliest copy, and the actual number of manuscripts present in the world today as far we know. You will notice that the first sentence of this paragraph is more than justified by the data.

Works	Date Written	Earliest Copy	#Manuscripts
Aristotle's poetics	384-322 B.C	1100 A.D	49
Plato's tetralogies	427-347 B.C	900 A.D.	7
Herodotus	488-428 B.C.	900 A.D.	8
Tacitus	100 A.D.	1100 A.D.	20
Thucydides	460-400 B.C.	900 A.D.	8
Homer's Iliad	800 B.C.	400 B.C.	643
Caesar's Gallic War	58-50 B.C.	900 A.D.	10
Livy Roman History	59 B.C.-17 A.D.	900 A.D.	20
New Testament	48-95 A.D.	200 A.D	5,500+
Old Testament	1500-400 B.C.	125 B.C.	1,000+

The manuscript evidence is taken from the first edition of Josh McDowell, *Evidence that Demands a Verdict*, Campus Crusade for Christ, Arrowhead Springs, Ca.1972, p.48. He cites F.W.Hall, ``MS Authorities for the Text of the Chief Classical Writers`` in *Companion to Classical Text* (Oxford at the Clarendon Press, 1913) for the Greek and Roman manuscript evidence. The New Testament figures are conservative and do not include either New Testament fragments from before 200 A.D. or the vast number of early translations such as Syriac, Old Latin, et al. The Old Testament manuscript evidence includes Dead Sea Scroll material including two copies of Isaiah - 1QIs.A and 1QIs.B.

Though citing a 1913 source for classical writers may seem outdated, this would be misleading since there have not been numerically significant new discoveries of Greek or Roman manuscripts since that date.

No scholar seriously questions the integrity of these classical texts. The reason is simple. Though centuries have elapsed between the original writing and the earliest extant copy, scholars are satisfied that with a number of manuscripts to compare one with another they can have confidence they are reading what, for example, Plato or Caesar wrote.

The New Testament textual evidence is overwhelming both in time elapsed between original composition and earliest extant copies as well as the high number of manuscripts. It is absolutely irrational to question the reliability of the text when scholars with far less data available would never question the integrity of other works.

A Final Word: God, Stephen Hawking and Me

I have found that in trusting Christ, He has proven Himself to be a gracious Saviour. I mentioned earlier that I have A.L.S. As a result, I have no ability to manipulate my fingers. This document has been word processed using two prostheses, one on each hand that enables me to peck at the keyboard letter by letter. I can no longer stand or walk. I do not say these things to evoke sympathy. I say them to show that in the darkest times Christ's light shines brightly. He truly does give peace and joy that transcends the circumstances of life.

Fellow A.L.S. patient, Stephen Hawking, has recently said that faith in Christ and the hope of Heaven are crutches to make us feel comfortable in the universe. I argue just the opposite. The atheistic Darwinian worldview is a crutch to convince ourselves that we are not accountable to God and need not fear His judgment.

The beauty of trusting Christ is that I no longer need fear the judgment of God since Christ has taken my place and absorbed the wrath due me into Himself. He not only forgives our sins but He transforms our very being through the power of His Holy Spirit. I commend Him to you.

APPENDIX -
THE MEANING OF *yôm* IN GENESIS 1:1-2:4

THE QUESTION OFTEN ARISES AS TO THE CORRECT MEANING OF 'DAY' IN the opening verses of Genesis. There are those who argue that the word signifies a long period of time (e.g. progressive creationists like Hugh Ross). Others contend that the passage in question (Genesis 1:2-2:4) is not meant to be an actual historical account of the creation but is rather a theological reflection on God's creative power and His sovereignty over the created order (e.g. the 'framework hypothesis' of Meredith Kline, Henri Blocher *et al.*). In the latter case the text is seen as having no relevance in determining the sequence of events at the time of origins.

The traditional view has been that the text is meant to communicate a straightforward account of God's creation of the universe. The account is, therefore, of six 24-hour days of creative acts followed by a seventh 24-hour day of divine rest.

THEOLOGICAL REFLECTION APPROACH:
Regarding this approach it is important to note that it is *not* really a question of Hebrew textual exegesis but rather a hermeneutical conclusion driven by factors *external to the text*. Taking the 'framework hypothesis' as an example, at an initial glance, Days 1–3 seem to be showing the creation of three empty 'realms' or 'domains' and Days 4–6 showing the creation of their respective 'kings' or 'rulers'. Even if this was true, it would simply inform us that God created the universe in a specific order

of divine acts. It would not annul the historicity of the account unless the reader felt compelled for other reasons to see the pattern as purely literary.[1] In fact the structure of Genesis 1:1–2:4 does not really lend itself fully to the schema. For further details the reader is invited to consider the analyses of Wayne Grudem [2] and Jonathan Sarfati. [3]

Poetry or prose?

A question arises as to the genre of the passage: is it poetry or is it prose narrative? If it is poetry, then perhaps there is greater flexibility in the meaning of the words. If it is prose narrative, then it would be appropriate to read it as intending to give a historical account of the creation.

Regarding the issue of genre, even if it is poetry, the passage would not necessarily be overly flexible in its interpretation. Psalm 78 is clearly poetic and yet gives an accurate account of Israel's history from the Exodus to the anointing of David.

Furthermore, it can be easily demonstrated that Genesis 1:1-2:4 in fact is not a poem. Hebrew poetry is characterized by certain syntactical features. A thorough grammatical/syntactical treatment of Hebrew poetry is that of M. O'Connor.[4] A simple test is the use of parallelism where a second grammatical clause repeats the idea of the preceding clause either by way of rewording it, or further explicating it, or by expressing its antithesis. O'Connor's analysis goes far beyond these simple observations but does not nullify them. Reading the Hebrew text shows that it lacks these requisite poetic markers. Therefore, the Hebrew text is most reasonably read as prose narrative.

Secondly (and more objectively), in prose narrative there is a different ratio of verbal forms than there is in poetry. This has long been recognized by Hebrew scholars and has most recently been exhaustively analyzed by Steven Boyd.[5] By way of explanation there are four forms of the finite verb in biblical Hebrew: the preterit (*vayyiqtol*), the imperfect (*yiqtol*), the perfect (*qatal*) and the *vav* perfect (*veqatal*). To quickly summarize, in passages that are universally recognized as historical narrative there is a marked preponderance of preterits over the other three forms. In poetry there is a preponderance of imperfects (*yiqtol*) and perfects (*qatal*).

APPENDIX

Boyd demonstrates that, given the ratio of verbal forms, the statistical evidence for the text being prose is overwhelming. Indeed it would be irresponsible to read it any other way.

The use of the word *yôm* in Genesis 1:1-2:4 with particular reference to the use of the cardinal number ***echad*** in 1:5b:

Regarding the word '*yôm*' in Genesis 1:1-2:4, it is apparent that there are three different uses of the term in the passage. In 1:5a it denotes 'daylight' as opposed to 'night'. In 1:5b it denotes the combination of the two. The word '*echad*' is most probably to be read as a cardinal number ('one') as opposed to an ordinal ('first') in contrast to many translations. Thus it appears that the text is in fact defining what a 'day' is in the rest of the Creation Week. Finally in Genesis 2:4 *yôm* is part of an anarthrous[6] prepositional compound *b'yôm* meaning not 'in the day' but simply 'when'.

The fact that for the bulk of the passage, the word *yôm* is accompanied by sequential numerical denotation and the language of 'evening and morning' gives a *prima facie* case that regular 24-hour days are in view.

Concerning the use of the cardinal as opposed to the ordinal in 1:5b, it will be helpful to examine this a little further. For a more detailed examination of *echad* in Genesis 1:5, the definitive study is that of Andrew Steinmann.[7] After examining *echad* as an ordinal number in numbering units of time he concludes that it may be used in place of the ordinal *r'ishon* in only two idioms: namely to 'designate the day of a month, the other the year of a reign of a king'.[8]

In addition, in a non temporal sense, the cardinal can stand for the ordinal when dealing with a small number of 'countable' items.[9]

In contrast, it has sometimes (often) been claimed that when a list of ordinal numbers is given, the cardinal form '*echad*' is to be rendered as an ordinal ('first').[10] BDB under usage #7 states 'as ordinal, *first*...'[11] and then cites Genesis 1:5, 2:11; Exodus 39:10; Ezekiel 10:14; Job 42:14 and then adds references to the *first* day of a month or *first* in a verbally compound ordinal number (thirty *first* ...).

This claim, as noted in the preceding comments, can be challenged. The word *echad* occurs 960 times in the Hebrew Old Testament.[12] In the AV it is rendered by the English 'first' a total of 32 times. The majority of these cases are part of a formulaic expression 'day one of the nth month'. Another cluster of ordinal renderings of *echad* is found in compound numbers, e.g., 'thirty-first year of Asa' (1Kings 16:23) (lit. 'in year of thirty and one of year'). These two clusters of citations are the very exceptions noted by Steinmann.

Another distinction that may be noted is that between simple 'countable'[13] lists and 'temporally sequential' events. To illustrate this distinction I will consider as examples of the former category five lists where the cardinal form (*echad*, 'one') is followed by ordinals ('second, third ... ') and can itself be considered as an ordinal.

1. Genesis 2:1: the list of the four heads of rivers flowing out of Eden follow this pattern.
2. Exodus 28:17: the same pattern is used to denote the four rows of jewels on the High Priest's breastplate.
3. Exodus 39:10-13: the same pattern appears, again in reference to the same article of clothing.
4. Ezekiel 10:14: the four heads of a cherub are enumerated in this way.
5. Job 42:14: the three daughters of Job are designated using this convention.

There are six other lists which share this same pattern.[14] Furthermore, in each of these cases the article is included. Steinmann concludes:

'The description of the use of *echad* as an ordinal number for the first element in a small number of countable items should state: *With a definite noun,* echad *serves (as an ordinal) to count the first of a small number of things. In this construction the noun may be elided after a recent mention,* [but] *the article is never omitted from the adjective or its governing noun. The following items are counted with ordinal numbers.*'[15]

In effect, this means that when *echad* is unaccompanied by the article and used adjectively it is reasonable that it be considered as a cardinal ('one'). Some may challenge this conclusion claiming that it may be an example of 'denying the antecedent' but it does seem to have merit.[16]

Another observation is that in lists, which particularly stress sequential events, the ordinal *r'ishon* ('first') is used. I consider six such occasions:

APPENDIX

1. Numbers 7:12-89 gives the offerings of the twelve tribal leaders on succeeding days. The first day uses the ordinal *r'ishon*. This text illustrates another feature, namely that once you reach the compound Hebrew numbers (11 and up) the terms are in the cardinal form.[17]
2. Numbers 28:16: *r'ishon* is used to describe the first day of unleavened bread. In verse 25 the text refers to the seventh (ordinal) day of the feast. Intervening ordinals are not present in verses 17–24.
3. 1 Chronicles 24:7-18: the sequence of 24 lots is cast for the divisions of the priesthood who serve in successive order. Again the ordinal *r'ishon* is used to begin the sequence.
4. 1 Chronicles 25:9-31 gives a similar sequential ordering of the 24 families of temple singers and *r'ishon* is used to commence the list.
5. 1 Chronicles 27:2-15 gives the monthly rotation of David's 12 army divisions (24,000 men per division) who served in sequence throughout the year. The ordinal *r'ishon* is used for the first division.
6. Zechariah 6:2-3 lists the four angelic chariots are listed but it appears from the text that they are coming out from between the two mountains, possibly in temporal order. This latter point depends on whether they are pictured as emerging in single file and not coming out four abreast. I would tend to opt for the former since *r'ishon* is used instead of *echad*. Nevertheless, certainty eludes us in this case.

From this survey it does appear that a list emphasizing a temporal sequence of events tends to commence with the ordinal *r'ishon* as opposed to the cardinal *echad* which we found employed in the five lists of 'countable items' (plus the further six cited in the endnote).

Given that Genesis 1 is describing a sequence of creative acts one would expect to find the first day designated by the ordinal *r'ishon*. Instead, we find the cardinal form *echad*. From the preceding overview of lists it would seem clear that this initial appearance of the cardinal form is in fact signifying a cardinal meaning.

155

Furthermore, both *echad* and *yôm* are without the article indicating that the expression denotes 'one day'. In fact the article does not appear until the sixth day - *yôm hašišiy.*

Steinmann comments:

'But even here the grammar is strange, since there is no article on *yôm,* as would be expected. This would indicate that the sixth day was a regular solar day, but that it was *the culminating day of creation.* Likewise, the seventh day is referred to as *yôm hašebi'iy* (Genesis 2:3), with lack of an article on *yôm.* This also, the author is implying, was a regular solar day. Yet it was a special day, because God had finished his work of creation.'[18]

An additional comment to Steinmann's which I believe reinforces his point is that the prefix *beth* attached to *yôm* in Genesis 2:2a and 2:2b is both times pointed by the Massoretes with the *pathach,* implying the presence of the article. He is quite correct that in the concluding use of 'day the seventh' in Genesis 2:3b that *yôm* is anarthrous. Thus the pattern is actually:

Genesis:31: 'day the sixth'
Genesis 2:2a: 'in the day the seventh'
Genesis 2:2b: 'in the day the seventh'
Genesis 2:3: 'day the seventh'

This pattern highlights the peculiar nature of the concluding citation. Since the two prepositional phrases employ the expected use of the article, the fact that in the final reference the article is absent from *yôm* we are alerted to its uniqueness

Further emphasizing the special nature of the seventh day is the fact that it is the only one to have the day + ordinal occurring more than once.

In light of the preceding, it is clearly preferable to read 1:5b as defining a *yôm* for the following sequence of ordinals-namely one cycle of evening and morning, signifying a complete 24-hour day embracing both the period of darkness and the period of light. Having used the cardinal *echad* to establish that definition of *yôm,* the chapter then goes on in the expected ordinal sequence.

Appendix

The only other passage in the entire Bible that makes reference to the Creation Week as a six-day sequence followed by a seventh day of rest is Exodus 20:8-11, where a one to one correspondence is seen between the regular 168 hour week of humans and God's work of creation and rest.

From the standpoint of Hebrew exegesis it is would be unreasonable to read another meaning into the text. The only reason for so doing would appear to be based on considerations other than a careful reading of the actual narrative.

Wenham (see endnote 1) and others hold that though the text clearly presents a sequence of six 24 hour days for the creation, the authorial intent is simply to show that "system and order... has been built into creation." He cites a number of literary features including "...the use of repeating formulae, the tendency to group words and phrases into tens and sevens, literary techniques such as chiasm and inclusion, the arrangement of creative acts into matching groups, and so on." In light of these literary phenomena he argues that Genesis 1 was never intended to be a straight forward historical narrative. Therefore, it should not be seen as in conflict with modern science (i.e., billions of years) but as complementary.

With all due respect I must observe that this reasoning is a classic example of *non sequitur*. It simply does not follow that literary elegance and sophistication preclude it from being a historical narrative. Wenham's reasoning would preclude the book of Esther from being historical. The NIV Study Bible gives a summary of compositional elegance in its introduction to Esther:

Banquets provide the setting for important plot developments. There are ten banquets: (1) 1:3–4, (2) 1:5–8, (3) 1:9, (4) 2:18, (5) 3:15, (6) 5:5–6, (7) 7:1–10, (8) 8:17, (9) 9:17, (10) 9:18. The three pairs of banquets that mark the beginning, middle and end of the story are particularly prominent: the two banquets given by Xerxes, the two prepared by Esther and the double celebration of Purim.

Recording duplications appears to be one of the favorite compositional techniques of the writer. In addition to the three groups of banquets that come in pairs there are two lists of the king's servants (1:10, 14), two reports that Esther concealed her identity (2:10, 20), two gatherings of women (2:8, 19), two fasts (4:3, 16), two consultations of Haman with his wife and friends (5:14; 6:13), two unscheduled appearances of Esther before the king (5:2; 8:3), two investitures for Mordecai (6:10–11; 8:15), two coverings of Haman's face (6:12; 7:8), two royal edicts (3:12–15; 8:1–14), two references to the subsiding of the king's anger (2:1; 7:10), two references to the irrevocability of the Persian laws (1:19; 8:8), two days for the Jews to take vengeance (9:5–12, 13–15) and two letters instituting the commemoration of Purim (9:20–28, 29–32).

Given this literary sophistication are we to jettison Esther's historical validity? Though many liberal scholars have no difficulty doing that, I am not sure Wenham, Kline, Blocher, Sailhamer, Waltke, Walton et al would concur (at least I hope not.)

Indeed there are three broad genres that have a different authorial intent than appears in the text: the modern realistic novel, parables, and ironic literature.

The modern realistic novel (e.g. John Grisham) presents a narrative that could be real and if one did not know the genre one would assume that the characters and events were real. His book *The Innocent Man* is actually a historical account of a wrongful conviction for murder that Grisham investigated. The names and places are real. If the author did not inform the reader of this and if the case was not a matter of public record, one would think they were reading a typical Grisham legal thriller. Yet it reads much like his fictional works. This illustrates the believability of the genre in that it is difficult to distinguish it from reality and vice versa.

Parables, particularly those of our Lord, tell stories from everyday life experiences, most of which could take place. Nevertheless, they are not meant to be seen as actual events but as an 'earthly' story to make a spiritual point.

Ironic literature would include such masterpieces as Jonathan Swift's *A Modest Proposal* where the 'economist proposer' advocates the selling of Irish children for food to grace the tables of the rich. Swift published it anonymously in 1729 as a biting satire on the English landlords' grinding oppression of the Irish tenant farmers. Many people were outraged at the pamphlet, thinking that someone was actually proposing infanticide and cannibalism. The point was to show the brutal conditions among the poor and to awaken sympathy for them and not to treat them as commodities or animal stock.

The question arises, 'Is Genesis 1 a modern realistic novel?' The answer is clearly 'No.'

Is it a parable? Unlikely, since there is no indication given in the immediate context to indicate that it is such.

Is it a work of irony? If it is, then literary analysis is meaningless.

A FINAL OBSERVATION

It has been my experience that those who question the normal historical narrative reading of Genesis 1:1–2:4 tend to be my fellow evangelicals. Theological liberals recognize the text as saying that God created the universe in six 24-hour days. They see evangelicals who adopt alternative readings of the text as engaged in a form of suspect apologetics. I believe the liberal critique to be accurate. Where I differ from them, however, is that I believe the text is *correct* in what it is teaching. A more effective apologetic therefore lies in simply admitting what the text proclaims and showing that it has far more explanatory power than many people think. In that light, I am excited by the kind of research being conducted by creation science organizations. God means what He says and He did it just as Genesis says He did!

—Francis Humphrey, Ph.D.

Endnotes
to Appendix

[1] G. J. Wenham, *Genesis 1–15*, Word Biblical Commentary, (Waco, TX: Word Books, 1987). On p. 19 he states: '…"day". There can be little doubt that here "day" has its basic sense of a 24-hour period. The mention of morning and evening, the enumeration of the days, and the divine rest on the seventh show that a week of divine activity is being described here.' Then on p. 39 he contends, 'It has been unfortunate that one device which our narrative uses to express the coherence and purposiveness of the creator's work, namely, the distribution of the various creative acts to six days, has been seized on and interpreted over-literalistically, with the result that science and Scripture have been pitted against each other instead of being seen as complementary. Properly understood, Genesis justifies the scientific experience of unity and order in nature. The six-day schema is but one of several means employed in this chapter to stress the system and order that has been built into creation. Other devices include the use of repeating formulae, the tendency to group words and phrases into tens and sevens, literary techniques such as chiasm and inclusion, the arrangement of creative acts into matching groups, and so on.' In the main body of my text I point out that elegance of order and literary finesse do not preclude the historicity of a narrative account.

[2] W. Grudem, *Systematic Theology*, (Grand Rapids, MI: Zondervan, 1994), 302, 1994.

³J. Sarfati, *Refuting Compromise*, (Green Forest, AR: Master Books, 2004), 94-101.

⁴M. O'Connor,, *Hebrew Verse Structure*, (Winona Lake, Indiana: Eisenbrauns, 1980).

⁵Ibid.

⁶I.e. lacking the definite article. If the definite article (represented by the vowel marking *pathach* under the *beth*) then it would signify 'in the day'. Its lack signifies an idiomatic use meaning 'when' as in the NIV translation.

⁷A. Steinmann, "אֶחָד [echad] as an Ordinal Number and the Meaning of Genesis 1:5," *Journal of the Evangelical Theological Societ*, 45, no. 4 (2002): 577-584.

⁸Ibid., 580.

⁹Ibid., 581–582.

¹⁰e.g. B. Davidson, *The Analytical and Chaldee Lexicon*, 8th printing. (Grand Rapids, MI: Zondervan Edition, 1976), 17. 'II *first*, only in the enumerating of time, where the cardinal stands for the ordinal.' He cites the usage when dealing with the first day (day one) of the nth month. See my comments in the main text.

¹¹F. Brown, C.A. Briggs, eds., *A Hebrew and English Lexicon of the Old Testament*, (UK: Oxford at the Clarendon Press, 1972), 25. Reprinted with corrections.

¹²R. L. Harris, G.L. Archer and B.K. Waltke, *Theological Word Book of the Old Testament*, Volume 1, (Chicago, IL: Moody Press, 1980), 30. This also corresponds to my count in Wigram, G.V., *The Englishman's Hebrew and Chaldee Concordance*, 7th printing. (Grand Rapids, MI: Zondervan Edition, 1978, where I counted 966.

¹³Steinmann, "Ordinal Number," 581; also B.K. Waltke and M.P. O'Connor, *An Introduction to Biblical Hebrew Syntax*, (Winona Lake, IN: Eisenbrauns, 1990), 274, § 15.2.1b.

¹⁴Genesis 4:19: 'the *name of the first* [of two wives] *was Adah*'; Exodus 26:4,5; 36:11: '*the first curtain*' [of two]; Exodus 29:40, Numbers 28:7: '*for the first lamb*' [of two]; 1Kings 6:24: '*the first cherub*' In each case *echad* is followed by ordinal forms (*second, third* ...).

[15] Steinmann, "Ordinal Number," 562. This is a refinement (indeed, correction) of Waltke and O'Connor's treatment.

[16] 'Denying the antecedent', i.e.
a) *echad* with the article signifies an ordinal use.
b) In this text *echad* does not have the article.
c) Therefore, in this text *echad* has a cardinal use.

'Denying the antecedent' since the premise does not assert that an ordinal use of *echad* necessarily has the article. However, in this case it is still reasonable to take it as a cardinal usage since the default meaning of *echad* is cardinal. Its ordinal usage is apparent from the context and in these cases the article is always present. Context shows that in the vast majority of cases the default cardinal meaning is implied and in those cases the article is missing. For the few cases where the meaning may be disputed, the burden of proof lies with those who would challenge the regular pattern. I note this mild caveat since Steinmann (see above) does maintain that the ordinal use is always accompanied by the article. Therefore, *he would restate the premise* as: *a)* *echad* with, and only with, the article signifies an ordinal use; b) and c) would, therefore, logically follow. I believe Steinmann is correct and I simply note a mild objection that might conceivably be raised.

[17] Actually 'eleven' is interesting in that it uses *'ashtēy* in construct with the cardinal *'asar* ('ten'). The etymology is uncertain and is only found in the plural construct form attached to 'ten'.

[18] Steinmann, "Ordinal Number," 583-584.

Endnotes to the
Main Text of Origins and Redemption

[1] The fact of light in verse 3 being created on the first day prior to the creation of the sun, moon and stars on the fourth day was addressed by Calvin: "It did not, however, happen from inconsideration or by accident, that the light preceded the sun and the moon. To nothing are we more prone than to tie down the power of God to those instruments the agency of which he employs. The sun and moon supply us with light: And, according to our notions we so include this power to give light in them, that if they were taken away from the world, it would seem impossible for any light to remain. Therefore the Lord, by the very order of the creation, bears witness that he holds in his hand the light, which he is able to impart to us without the sun and moon. Further, it is certain from the context that the light was so created as to be interchanged with darkness." Retrieved from http://www.ccel.org/ccel/calvin/calcom01.vii.i.html(Christian Classics Etherial Library).

[2] Francis Humphrey, "The Meaning of YÔM in Genesis1:1-2:4," *Journal of Creation* 21, **no.** 2 (2007): 52-55. See Appendix above.

James Stambaugh, "The Days of Creation: A Semantic Approach," *TJ* (now *Journal of Creation*) 5no.1(1991):70-78.

[3] Based on the "very good" divine verdict of Genesis 1:31 and the fact that Col. 1:16 includes the angelic realm in the creation along with the physical universe. Therefore, the 'un-good' rebellion must have been after the seventh day.

[4] "Devil" *diabolos* is the Greek equivalent.

[5] Tim Lovett, "Which Cubit for Noah's ARK?" *Journal of Creation* 20, no. 3 (December 2006): 71-77, http://creation.com/images/pdfs/tj/j20_3/j20_3_71-77.pdf.

[6] John Woodmorappe: *Noah's Ark: A Feasibility Study*, (El Cajon, California: Institute for Creation Research, 1996), 10-13. He estimates 8000 genera, extinct and present, each representing a "kind" (Heb. *min*). If the "kind" more often corresponded to the taxonomic category of 'family' then the number would be much lower. Later it will be demonstrated that only land dwelling vertebrates were on the ark – including dinosaurs.

[7] I take Genesis 9:27 (*pace* NIV) to mean *but He (God) will dwell in the tents of Shem* taking the *vav* to be adversative and the 3rd person actor to be God and not Japheth. Furthermore, in Genesis 12:3, Abraham, a descendant of Shem is told by God that, through Abraham, all the nations of the world would be blessed.

[8] Not all evolutionary cosmologists accept the 'hot big bang'. 'Steady state' cosmology has enjoyed a bit of a revival. See: Fred Hoyle, Geoffrey Burbidge and Jayant V. Narlikar, *A Different Approach to Cosmology*, (Cambridge: Cambridge University Press, 2000). Review by John Hartnett retrievable @ http://creation.com/images/pdfs/tf/j16_1/j16_1_29-35.pdf

[9] J. Hutton, *Theory of the Earth with Proof and Illustrations*, in A. Holmes, *Principles of Physical Geology* 2nd edition, (London: Thomas Nelson & Sons, 1965), 43, j.woodmorappe http://creation.com/hypercanes.

[10] Tom Hogan, "Some Implications of the Demise of the Demarcation Problem," *CRSQ* 46, no. 3 (Winter 2010): 167-176. http://www.creationresearch.org/crsq/articles/46/46_3/CRSQ%20Winter%202010%20Hogan.pdf.

[11] Francesco Fornai, Patrizia Longone, Luisa Cafaro, Olga Kastsiuchenka, Michela Ferrucci, Maria Laura Manca, Gloria Lazzeri, Alida Spalloni, Natascia Bellio, Paola Lenzi, Nicola Modugno, Gabriele Siciliano, Ciro Isidoro, Luigi Murri, Stefano Ruggieri, and Antonio Paparelli, "Lithium delays progression of amyotrophic lateral sclerosis,"

Proceedings of the National Academy of Sciences 105, no.6 (February 2008): 2052-2057. doi:10.1073/pnas.0708022105.

[12] Larry Vardiman, PhD, Andrew A. Snelling PhD, Eugene F. Chaffin, PhD, eds., *Radioisotopes and the Age of the Earth* Vol. II (El Cajon California: ICR, 2005) 25-100. These results were also published in: D.R. Humphreys, S.A. Austin, J.R. Baumgardner, and A.A. Snelling, "Recently measured helium diffusion rate for zircon suggests inconsistency with U-Pb age for Fenton Hill granodiorite," *Eos, Transactions of the American Geophysical Union* 84, no. 46, (2003). Fall Meet. Suppl., Abstract V32C-1047.

[13] Eugene F. Chafin, "Accelerated Decay: Theoretical Considerations," *RATE II: Radioisotopes and the Age of The Earth: Results of a Young-Earth Creationist Research Initiative,* eds., L. Vardiman et al, (San Diego, CA: Institute for Creation Research and the Creation Research Society, 2005), 525-586.

[14] Ibid., 101-208.

[15] Dr. Werner Gitt, *In the Beginning was Information,* trans, JaapKies, (Arizona: Master Books, 2000), provides a thorough presentation of information theory.

[16] A. Einstein, "Remarks on Russell's theory of knowledge," in *The Philosophy of Bertrand Russell,* ed., P. A. Schilpp, (New York: Tudor. 1944), 277-291.

[17] I heard this in an interview on CBC Montreal Radio many years ago.

[18] Robert W. Carter, "Can Mutations Create New Information?" http://creation.com/mutations-new-information.

[19] Jonathan Sarfati, "Origin of Life: instability of building blocks," *Journal of Creation* 13 no. 2 (November 1999): 124-127, gives a brief and knowledgeable critique of the RNA world hypothesis.

[20] "Origins of Life Prize." Last modified October, 2012, http://www.us.net/life/rul_abou.htm.

[21] David L. Abel and Jack T. Trevors, "Self-organization vs. self-ordering events in life-origin models," *Physics of Life Reviews* 3, no. 4 (December 2006): 211-228, http://dx.doi.org/10.1016/j.plrev.2006.07.003.

²² Karl R. Popper, ``Scientific Reduction and the Essential Incompleteness of All Science," in *Studies in the Philosophy of Biology*, eds., F. Iin Ayala, and T. Dobzhansky, (Berkeley: University of California Press, 1974), 270.

²³ Jonathan Sarfati, *TJ* (now *Journal of Creation*) 12, no. 3 (December 1998): 263–266, http://creation.com/origin-of-life-the-chirality-problem and 281-284, http://creation.com/origin-of-life-the-polymerization-problem. Physical chemist Sarfati outlines two chemical roadblocks (among many): the chirality problem outlined by physical chemist and the polymerization problem.

²⁴ J. C. Sanford, *Genetic Entropy & the Mystery of the Genome Third Edition*, (New York: FMS Publications, 2008).

²⁵ Ibid., 146. The quotation is an Author's Note and italicized in the original as is the **bold** writing.

²⁶ Susumu Ohno, *Evolution of Genetic Systems*, ed. H.H. Smith, (New York: Gordon and Breach, 1972), 366-370. So much "junk DNA in our genome. Also see L.E. Orgel, and F.H. Crick, "Selfish DNA: the ultimate parasite," *Nature* 284, no. 5757 (April 1980): 604-607. Both of these citations were found in Wikipedia under "Noncoding DNA."

²⁷ ENCODE Project Consortium, "Identification and analysis of functional elements in 1% of the human genome by the ENCODE pilot project," *Nature* 447, (June 14, 2007):799–816. The main site for the project is http://www.genome.gov/10005107.

²⁸ From a transcript of the ABC TV science program *Catalyst*, episode titled "Genius of Junk (DNA)," broadcast 10 July 2003, www.abc.net.au/catalyst/stories/s898887.htm.

²⁹ Jerry Coyne: *Why Evolution is True*, (New York: Penguin, 2009), 55-84.

³⁰ Y. Inai, Y. Ohta, and M. Nishikimi, *J. Nutritional Science and Vitaminology* 49, no. 5 (2003): 315-319, http://www.journalarchive.jst.go.jp/jnlpdf.php?cdjournal=jnsv1973&cdvol=49&noissue=5&startpage=315&lang=en&from=jnltoc. "The whole structure of the human non-functional L-gulono-γ³-lactone oxidase gene—the gene responsible for scurvy—and the evolution of repetitive sequences thereon."

[31] John Woodmorappe, "Potentially decisive evidence against pseudogene 'shared mistakes.'" *Journal of Creation* 18 no. 3 (December 2004): 63–69, http://creation.com/potentially-decisive-evidence-against-pseudogene-shared-mistakes.

[32] Lee Spetner, *Not by Chance*. (Brooklyn: The Judaica Press, 1997). Biophysicist L. Spetner gives a compelling case for this position.

[33] H. J. Muller, "Our load of mutations," *American Journal of Human Genetics* 2 (1950): 111-176. http://www.ncbi.nlm.nih.gob/pmc/articles/PMC1716299/pdf/ajhg004299-0003.pdf.

[34] Ibid., 71, 72.

[35] A. S. Kondrashov, "Contamination of the genome by very slightly deleterious mutations: why have we not died 100 times over?" *Journal of Theoretical Biology* 175 (1995): 583-594. In personal communication he has informed Dr. Sanford that the number may be as high as 300. Sanford, *Genetic Entropy*. A mutation rate of 300 per human genome means 300 per 3,000,000,000 base pairs, or 1 in 10 million. See feedback article by Don Batten at http://creation.com/bacterial-mutations-plus-biblical-geology.

[36] Alex Williams, "Mutations: evolution's engine becomes evolution's end!" *Journal of Creation* 22, no. 2 (August 2008): 60-66.

[37] Delft University of Technology, "Real-time Observation Of DNA-repair Mechanism," *ScienceDaily*, (May 25, 2008): http://www.sciencedaily.com/releases/2010/10/101004112156.htm and the abstract of "An unprecedented nucleic acid capture mechanism for excision of DNA damage," *Nature* 468 (November 18, 2010): 406-411, http://www.sciencedaily.com/releases/2008/05/080522120610.htm.

[38] Carl Wieland, "Creationist article 'saved my favourite cow,'" (November 1, 2008): http://creation.com/creationist-article-saved-my-favorite-cow. E.g. the bacterium has an enzyme that usually has a useful purpose, but it also turns an antibiotic into a poison. So a mutation disabling this enzyme would render the antibiotic harmless. But this bacterium is still disabled, because the useful process the enzyme usually enables is now hindered, so it would be unable to compete in the wild with non-resistant ones. The information loss in...the bacterium is the *opposite* of what evolution requires.

[39] Jerry Bergman, "Does gene duplication provide the engine for evolution?" *Journal of Creation* 20, no. 1 (April 2006): 99-104. http://creation.com/does-gene-duplication-provide-the-engine-for-evolution.

[40] S. Ohno, *Evolution by Gene Duplication*, (Berlin: Springer-Verlag, 1970). W. H. Li, *Molecular Evolution*, (Sunderland, MA: Sinauer Associates, 1997), 269.

[41] G.S. Eakin and R.R. Behringer, "Tetraploid development in the mouse," *Developmental Dynamics* 228 (2003):751–766.

[42] Bergman, "Does gene duplication provide the engine for evolution?"

[43] Chromatid, http://www.biology-online.org/dictionary/Centromere The duplication is caused by a faulty centromere: "When the centromere is not functioning properly, the chromatids do not align and separate properly, thus, resulting in the wrong number of chromosomes in the daughter cells, and conditions such as Down syndrome." Chromatid: "Either of the two strands joined together by a single centromere, formed from the duplication of the chromosome during the early stages of cell division and then separate to become individual chromosomes during the late stages of cell division."

[44] Jeffrey Tomkins and Jerry Bergman, "The chromosome 2 fusion model of human evolution – part 1: re-evaluating the evidence and part 2: re-analysis of the genomic data," *Journal of Creation* 25, no. 2 (2011): 106-117. This excursus is a brief summary of this article.

[45] *Merriam-Webster Online,* s.v. "pongid," accessed November 3, 2012, http://www.merriam-webster.com/dictionary/%3A Defined as: any of a family (Pongidae) of apes that includes the chimpanzee, gorilla, and orangutan.

[46] D.J. Fairbanks, *Relics of Eden,* (Amherst, NY: Prometheus Books, 2007), quoted in Tomkins and Bergman, "Chromosome 2," 106-107.

[47] J. Devanshi, and J. P. Promisel, "Telomeric Strategies: Means to an End," *Annual Review of Genetics* 44 (2010): 243-269. http://www.annualreviews.org/doi/full/10.1146/annurev-genet-102108-13484. Quoted in Tomkins and Bergman, 108.

[48] Tomkins and Bergman, "Chromosome 2," 108.

⁴⁹ Basic Local Alignment Search Tool Nucleotide – an algorithm used to search a nucleotide database.

⁵⁰ Tompkins and Bergman, "Chromosome 2," 113.

⁵¹ Ibid., 116.

⁵² J.D. Seaman, and J.C. Sanford, J.C., Skittle, "A 2-dimensional genome visualization tool," *BMC Bioinformatics* 10, no. 452 (2009); and A. Baldini, et al. "An alphoid DNA sequence conserved in all human and great ape chromosomes: evidence for ancient centromeric sequences at human chromosomal regions 2q21 and 9q13," *Human Genetics* 90 (1993): 577-583. Quoted in Tomkins and Bergman, "Chromosome 2," 210.

⁵³ The Chimpanzee Sequencing and Analysis Consortium, "Initial sequence of the chimpanzee genome and comparison with the human genome," *Nature* 437 (2005): 69-87.Quoted in Tompkins and Bergman, "Chromosome 2," 114.

⁵⁴ Jeffrey P. Tomkins: "Genome-Wide DNA Alignment Similarity (Identity) for 40,000 Chimpanzee Sequences Queried against the Human Genome is 86% to 89%," insert *Answers Research Journal*, no. 4 (2011). http://www.answersingenesis.org/articles/arj/v4/n1/blastin.

⁵⁵ J.B.S. Haldane, "The Cost of Natural Selection," *Journal of Genetics*, no. 55 (1957). http://www.blackwellpublishing.com/ridley/classictexts/haldane2.pdf. A PDF of J.B.S. Haldane's 1957 paper.

⁵⁶ http://saintpaulscience.com/Haldane.htm

⁵⁷ Walter Remine, letter to *Journal of Creation* 23, no. 2 (2009): 65.

⁵⁸ Don Batten, "The adaptation of bacteria to feed on nylon waste," *Journal of Creation* 17, no. 3 (December 2003): 3-5. http://creation.com/the-adaptation-of-bacteria-to-feeding-on-nylon-waste. One such claim – bacterial mutation giving ability to ingest nylon is, upon examination, found to be quite dubious.

⁵⁹ Genesis 1 *passim*.

⁶⁰ Don Batten, "Ligers and Wholphins, What Next," *Creation* 22, no. 3 (June 2003): 28-33. http://creation.com/ligers-and-wholphins-what-next.

⁶¹ Ibid.

⁶² Ibid.

⁶³ The Darwin Correspondence Project, letter no. 2814, accessed December 25, 2010, http://www.darwinproject.ac.uk/entry-2814/.

⁶⁴ The Darwin Correspondence Project, accessed November 7, 2012, http://www.darwinproject.ac.uk/correspondence-with-asa-gray.

⁶⁵ Approximately 300 letters written between 1854 and 1881.

⁶⁶ Darwin Correspondence Project Database, letter no. 12041, accessed December 26, 2010, http://www.darwinproject.ac.uk /entry-12041/.

⁶⁷ F. Darwin, ed., *The life and letters of Charles Darwin, including an autobiographical chapter,* (London: John Murray, 1887), 77. http://darwin-online.org.uk. Darwin and Lyell became good friends and it was Lyell who urged Darwin to publish the *Origin*.

⁶⁸ He is referring to: "Loa Loa worms (also known as the "eye worm") are classified as filarial worms, meaning they thrive in human tissue. The Loa Loa worm is also called the "eye worm" because they often migrate through the eye and surrounding subsurface areas. At one time, prior to the 1920s, loaloa worm infections occurred in the United States. Today, however, they mainly infect people who are native to Sudan, and those who live in or near Central and West Africa's swamps and rain forests. Loiasis is the infestation of loaloa worms in humans. The larvae are first collected from an infected individual when a mango fly (horsefly) or a deer fly bites the individual, and acquires the larvae. The larvae then progress through the fly's body, finally reaching the feeding tube. They are then transferred to a human host when the fly bites the human." Available at: http://allaboutworms.com/loa-loa-eye-worm. Significantly, Christian organizations, many of whose staff are ardent creationists, are in the forefront of combating this and other diseases, in the developing world.

⁶⁹ David Attenborough, "Attenborough reveals creationist hate mail for not crediting God," *The Guardian* (January 2009):, http://www.guardian.co.uk/world/2009/jan/27/david-attenborough-science.

⁷⁰ I take the Greek word *ktisis* (creation) in this context to mean "the universe."

⁷¹ Shaun Doyle, personal communication, accessed November 17, 2012.

⁷² Jerry Bergman, George Howe, "Vestigial Organs Are Fully Functional," *Creation Research Society Monograph Series,* no. 4 (1990.

⁷³ See above remarks on ENCODE. See also Ewen Callaway, "'Junk' DNA gets credit for making us who we are," (March 19, 2010): http://www.newscientist.com/article/dn18680-junk-dna-gets-credit-for-making-us-who-we-are.html. "In recent years, researchers have recognised that non-coding DNA, which makes up about 98 per cent of the human genome, plays a critical role in determining whether genes are active or not and how much of a particular protein gets churned out."

⁷⁴ K. Franze, *et al.*, Müller, "Cells are living optical fibers in the vertebrate retina," *Proc. Nat. Acad. Sci. USA,* 10.1073/pnas.0611180104, no.7(May 2007. www.pnas.org/cgi/content/abstract/0611180104v1. "We investigated intact retinal tissue and individual Müller cells, which are radial glial cells spanning the entire retinal thickness. Müller cells have an extended funnel shape, a higher refractive index than their surrounding tissue, and are oriented along the direction of light propagation. Transmission and reflection confocal microscopy of retinal tissue *in vitro* and *in vivo* showed that these cells provide a low-scattering passage for light from the retinal surface to the photoreceptor cells. Using a modified dual-beam laser trap we could also demonstrate that individual Müller cells act as optical fibers. Furthermore, their parallel array in the retina is reminiscent of fiberoptic plates used for low-distortion image transfer. Thus, Müller cells seem to mediate the image transfer through the vertebrate retina with minimal distortion and low loss. This finding elucidates a fundamental feature of the inverted retina as an optical system and ascribes a new function to glial cells." **This utterly destroys the dysteleological argument re the vertebrate eye.**

⁷⁵ Jerry Bergman, "Is the human pharynx poorly designed?" *Journal of Creation,* 22, no. 1 (2008).41-43. The following is taken from p.42"The pharynx design allows both simultaneous eating and breathing with greater efficiency and less body bulk than if we had two separate unconnected channels. Importantly, one cannot breathe and swallow at

the same time, effectively separating the two systems. The two separate systems also function exceptionally well because unconscious reflexes, in the absence of disease, allows them to function without concern or worry for most of our life. Critics argue, without empirical evidence, that completely separate tube systems, one for respiration and another for the alimentary tract, would be a superior design. This design, though, some argue based on knowledge of anatomy and logic, would require a far more complex tube and networking system, resulting in a greater likelihood for errors and casualties. Two systems would have to be coordinated so they could operate separately."

[76] Hideki Endo, DaishiroYamagiwa, Yoshihiro Hayashi, Hiroshi Koie, Yoshiki Yamaya, Junpei Kimura, "Role of the giant panda's pseudo-thumb," *Nature*, 347 (January 28, 1999): 309-310. "The radial sesamoid bone and the accessory carpal bone form a double pincer-like apparatus in the medial and lateral sides of the hand, respectively, enabling the panda to manipulate objects **with great dexterity**." (emphasis added) They go on to say ""[t]he way in which the giant panda ... uses the radial sesamoid bone -- its 'pseudo-thumb' -- for grasping makes it one of the most extraordinary manipulation systems in mammalian evolution." And yet the panda's thumb is still referred to by many as 'poorly designed.'

[77] Not only by ENCODE but more recently by Laura Poliseno, Leonardo Salmena, Jiangwen Zhang, Brett Carver, William J. Haveman & Pier Paolo Pandolfi, "Acoding-independent function of gene and pseudogene mRNAs regulates tumour biology," *Nature* 465, no. 1033–1038(24 June 2010): doi:10.1038/nature09144 Editor's Summary:A role for pseudogenes: MicroRNAs are known to regulate gene expression by interacting with incompletely complementary sequences in a target messenger RNA. But is the converse true: can mRNA expression affect the distribution of miRNAs? A new study shows that the 3′untranslated region of a pseudogene — the tumour suppressor pseudogene *PTENP1* — can bind the same miRNAs as the related protein-coding gene, *PTEN*. This suggests that pseudogenes may have a biological function as 'decoys', sequestering miRNAs and thereby affecting their regulation of expressed genes.

[78] Jonathan Sarfati, *By Design: Evidence for nature's Intelligent Designer—the God of the Bible*, (Powder Springs, GA: Creation Book Publishers, 2008). This is an excellent creationist treatment of the subject, including interaction with the dysteleological argument.

[79] Another possibility is that such genetic potential was present in unexpressed form and only 'switched on' after the Fall. This would be consistent with God's omniscience and foreknowledge of Adam's decision.

[80] Including McGill (my Alma Mater) see http://barthelat-lab.mcgill.ca/.

[81] E.g. Isaiah 2:4 (NIV) "He will judge between the nations and will settle disputes for many peoples. They will beat their swords into plowshares and their spears into pruning hooks. Nation will not take up sword against nation, nor will they train for war anymore."

[82] Two centuries ago there were not the technologies and medical therapies that enable me, in spite of being confined to a wheel chair, still able to function - though obviously in a limited way!

[83] E.g., James Hannam, *God's Philosophers: How the Medieval World Laid the Foundations of Modern Science*, (U.K.: Icon Books Ltd., 2010).

[84] Peter Harrison, *The Fall of Man and the Foundations of Science*, (U.K: University of Oxford, 2007). http://www.cambridge.org/gb/knowledge/isbn/item1174484/?site_locale=en_GB#.

[85] Henry M. Morris and John C. Whitcomb, *The Genesis Flood: The Biblical Record and its Scientific Implications*, (Philadelphia: Presbyterian & Reformed Publishing, 1961). This is the title of the book that launched the modern creation science movement.

[86] Longevity of antediluvian population was probably (primarily) due to genetic factors with some environmental contribution affecting genetic decline. See Raúl E. López: http://creation.com/temporal-changes-in-the-ageing-of-biblical-patriarchs. See as well Sanford, 155.

[87] *Encyclopedia Britannica Online*, s.v. "Antonio Snider Pellegrini," accessed November 7, 2012, http://www.britannica.com/EBchecked/topic/550472/Antonio-Snider-Pellegrini.

⁸⁸ *New World Encyclopedia Online*, s.v. "Mid-ocean ridge," accessed November 7, 2012, http://www.newworldencyclopedia.org/entry/Mid-ocean_ridge.

⁸⁹ Sciencedaily.com, s.v. "Mid-ocean ridge," http://www.sciencedaily.com/articles/m/mid-ocean_ridge.htm.

⁹⁰ John R. Baumgardner, "Catastrophic Plate Tectonics: The Physics behind the Genesis Flood." Paper presented at International Conference on Creationism, Pittsburgh, PA, 2003. John R. Baumgardner, "Computer Modeling of the Large-Scale Tectonics Associated with the Genesis Flood." Paper presented at International Conference on Creationism, Pittsburgh, PA, 1994. John R. Baumgardner, "Runaway Subduction as the Driving Mechanism for the Genesis Flood." Paper presented at International Conference on Creationism, Pittsburgh, PA, 1994. http://www.globalflood.org. These papers are seminal works for this proposal.

⁹¹ Andrew A. Snelling, *Earth's Catastrophic Past, Geology, Creation and the Flood, Vol. 1 & 2*, (Dallas, TX: ICR, 2009). This is a major creation science work which gives a thorough treatment of earth's geological history with considerable treatment on catastrophic plate tectonics. The water jets are described on p. 697.

⁹² Michael J. Oard, "An impact Flood submodel – dealing with issues," *Journal of Creation* 26, no. 2 (2012): 73-81.

⁹³ Andrew A. Snelling, *Earth's Catastrophic Past, Geology, Creation and the Flood, Vol I & II*, (Dallas, TX: ICR, 2009). 697.

⁹⁴ A summary is found at Washington University in St. Louis News Release accessible at http://news.wustl.edu/news/Pages/8222.aspx The published article is "Earth's Deep Water Cycle," *Geophysical Monograph Series* 168 (2006), by the American Geophysical Union.10.1029/168GM19. http://epsc.wustl.edu/seismology/michael/web/LawrenceWysession_AGU_2006.pdf. A Creation Science response is by Emil Silvestru, "Water inside Fire," *JOURNAL OF CREATION*, 22, no. 1 (2008). http://creation.com/images/pdfs/tj/j22_1/j22_1_3-4.pdf.

⁹⁵ John R. Baumgardner, "Catastrophic Plate Tectonics: The Physics Behind the Genesis Flood." Paper presented at Fifth International Conference on Creationism (ICC), Pittsburgh, PA, August 4-8, 2003. http://www.globalflood.org/papers/2003ICCcpt.html.

⁹⁶ M. I. Budyko, A.B. Ronov, and A.L. Yanshin, *History of the Earth's Atmosphere*, (New York: Springer-Verlag, 1987), Tables 6 and 7, 59–62. Quoted in Roy D. Holt "Late Cainozoic Flood/post-Flood Boundary," *CEN Tech. J.*, 10, no. 1 (1996):14, 15. http://creation.com/images/journal_of_creation/vol10/v10n1_cainozoic.pdf.

⁹⁷ Roy D. Holt, "Late Cainozoic Flood/post-Flood Boundary," *CEN Tech J 10.*, no. 1 (1996): 141, http://creation.com/images/journal_of_creation/vol10/v101_cainozoic.pdf.

⁹⁸ John R. Baumgardner, "Catastrophic Plate Tectonics."

⁹⁹ Snelling, *Earth's Catastrophic Past* Vol 2, 693-694 summarizing Baumgardner ICC 2003 states: "Baumgardner presents numerical results, using a viscosity law that depends both on temperature and on stress, which show that slab runaway causes the effective viscosity of the entire volume of the mantle to plummet by orders of magnitude during the runaway episode. Therefore, motions throughout the mantle, far from the immediate vicinity of the slab, rise to values similar to that of the sinking slab itself."

¹⁰⁰ Baumgardner, ICC, 2003. "Such upwellings from the bottom boundary have dramatic implications for transient changes in sea level during the Flood since they produce a temporary rise in the height of the ocean bottom by several kilometers. Similarly, downwellings from the top boundary cause a temporary depression of the boundary. Because downwellings are generally beneath continental regions, they result in a temporary depression of the continental surfaces by similar amplitudes as the upwellings." The web paper is not paginated.

¹⁰¹ Andrew Snelling, "The 'principle of least astonishment'," *TJ* 9, no. 2 (August 1995): 138-139. http://creation.com/the-principle-of-least-astonishment. R.S. Coe, M. Prévot, and P. Camps, "New evidence for extraordinarily rapid change of the geomagnetic field during a reversal," *Nature* 374 (1995): 687-692. M. Prévot, E.A. Mankinen, C.S. Grommé, and R.S. Coe, "How the geomagnetic field vector reverses polarity," *Nature* 316 (1985): 230-234. E.A. Mankinen, M. Prévot, C.S. Grommé, and R.S. Coe, "The Steens Mountain (Oregon) geomagnetic polarity transition, 1. Directional variation, duration of episodes, and rock magnetism," *Journal of Geophysical Research,* 90 (1985): 10,393-

10,416. M. Prévot, E.A. Mankinen, R.S. Coe, and C.S. Grommé, "The Steens Mountain (Oregon) geomagnetic polarity transition, 2. Field intensity variations and discussion of reversal models," *Journal of Geophysical Research* 90 (1985): 10,417-10,448. R.S. Coe and M. Prévot, "Evidence suggesting extremely rapid field variation during a geomagnetic reversal." *Earth and Planetary Science Letters* 92 (1989): 292-298.

[102] D. Russell Humphreys, "Physical Mechanism for Reversals of the Earth's Magnetic Field During the Flood," Paper presented at the Second ICC, Pittsburgh, PA. July 30-August 4, 1990. Published in: R.E. Walsh & C.L. Brooks, eds., *Proceedings of the Second International Conference on Creationism*, (1990) 129-140. http://static.icr.org/i/pdf/technical/Physical-Mechanism-Reversals-of-Earths-Magnetic-Field.pdf.

[103] Tas Walker, "Grand Canyon strata show geologic time is imaginary," *Creation* 25, no. 1 (December 2002): 41, http://creation.com/grand-canyon-strata-show-geologic-time-is-imaginary. His note 1 is J.D. Morris: *The Young Earth*, (Arizona: Master Books, 1994):106-109.

[104] Jonathan D. Sarfati, "How did all the animals fit on the ark?," *The Creations Answers Book* (2006) 185, http://creation.com/images/pdfs/cabook/chapter 13.pdf. "With extinct genera, there is a tendency among some paleontologists to give each of their new finds a new genus name. But this is arbitrary, so the number of extinct genera is probably highly overstated. Consider the sauropods, which were the largest dinosaurs—the huge plant-eaters like Brachiosaurus, Diplodocus, Apatosaurus, etc. There are 87 sauropod genera commonly cited, but only 12 are 'firmly established' and another 12 are considered 'fairly well established'." Also citing: J.S. McIntosh, *Sauropoda*, (1992); D.B. Wieshampel, et al., *The Dinosauria*, (Berkeley, CA: University of California Press), 345.

[105] Until recently, tortoises were kept on board ships as a supply of fresh meat.

[106] Larry Pierce, "The Large Ships of Antiquity," *Creation ex nihilo* 22, no.3 (June 2000): 46-48, http://creation.com/the-large-ships-of-antiquity. Pierce gives documentation demonstrating that some of these

massive vessels were far larger than anything produced in the 18th or 19th centuries.

[107] Ken Ham, Tim Lovett, "Was There Really a Noah's Ark & Flood?" Accessed on November 10, 2012, http://www.answersingenesis.org/articles/nab/reall-a-flood-and-ark. The quote is found by clicking on #3 on the ark diagram.

[108] Athenaeus, *The Deipnosophists* 5, Section 203f–204b, describes a warship "built by Ptolemy Philopator (c. 244–205 BC). It was 130m (420 feet) long, 18m (57 feet) wide, and 22m (72 feet) high to the top of her gunwale. From the top of its sternpost to the water line was 24 metres (79.5 feet). It had four steering oars 14m (45 feet) long. It had 40 tiers of oars. [The 40 tiers could mean 20 for each of the two hulls if it was twin hulled. Ancient diagrams sometimes show the oar openings arranged diagonally thus saving vertical space]. The oars on the uppermost tier were 18m (57 feet) long. The oars were counterbalanced with lead to make them easier to handle. It had a double bow and a double stern and carried seven rams, of which one was the leader and the others were of gradually reducing size. It had 12 under-girders 275m (900 feet) long. The ship was manned by 400 sailors to handle the rigging and the sails, 4,000 rowers and 2,850 men in arms for a total of 7,250 men. This ship was too large to be of much practical use." Quoted in Larry Pierce, *Large Ships*.

[109] Jerry Coyne: *Why Evolution is True*, (NY: Penguin, 2009), 263.

[110] Morris and Whitcomb, *The Genesis Flood*.

[111] Snelling, *Earth's Catastrophic Past*.

[112] *TJ* now *Journal of Creation* 16, no. 1 (April 2002) http://creation.com?journal-of-creation-tj-161. The debate is found here and it consists of six papers, 3 pro CPT (John Baumgardner) and 3 anti CPT (Michael Oard). I have taken the 'pro' view since, in my mind, it seems to fit the evidence better.

[113] J. W. Hagadorn, R.H. Dott, and D. Damrow, "Stranded on a Late Cambrian shoreline: Medusae from central Wisconsin," *Geology* 30, no. 2 (2002): 147-150. Also see David Catchpoole: http://creation.com/hundreds-of-jellyfish-fossils.

[114] D. Fuchs, G. Bracchi, and R. Weis, "New octopods (Cephalopoda: Coleoidea) from the Late Cretaceous (Upper Cenomanian) of Hâkel and Hâdjoula, Lebanon," *Palaeontology* 52, no. 1 (2009): 65-81. See also: "Rare fossil octopuses found," LiveScience.com (March 18, 2009). http://www.livescience.com/animals/090318-fossil-octopus.html.

[115] Garry Graham, "Fast octopus fossils reveal no evolution. Accessed on November 10, 2012, http://creation.com/fast-octopus-fossils.

[116] R. Zangerl and E.S. Richardson, "The paleoecological history of two Pennsylvanian black shales," *Fieldiana: Geology Memoirs* 4 (1963). Quoted in http://creation.com/green-river-blues.

[117] "'Barren' Seafloor Teeming With Microbial Life," last modified May 29, 2008, www.sciencedaily.com/releases/2008/05/080528140303.htm. 'Barren' seafloor teeming with microbial life.

[118] Philip J. Currie and Eva B. Koppelhus, *101 Questions about Dinosaurs,* (Dover Publications, 1996). http://creation.com/dinosaur-bonesjust-how-old-are-they-really. Currie is a well-known dinosaur authority. He is Curator of Dinosaurs at the Royal Tyrrell Museum of Palaeontology, Drumheller, Alberta, Canada. Koppelhus is a visiting researcher at the same institution.

[119] J.R. Baumgardner, "John R. Baumgardner: Geophysics" Accessed on November 10, 2012. http://creation.com/john-r-baumgardner-geophysics-in-six-days.

[120] J.R. Baumgardner and D.W. Barnette, Patterns of Ocean Circulation Over the Continents During Noah's Flood; in: R.E. Walsh (Ed.), *Proceedings of the Third International Conference on Creationism, Technical Symposium Sessions,* Creation Science Fellowship, Inc., Pittsburgh, PA, 1994. 77–86.

[121] Steven A. Austin, *Grand Canyon: Monument to Catastrophe* (Santee, CA: Institute for Creation Research, Santee, 1994), 75.

[122] Andrew Snelling. "Transcontinental Rock Layers: Flood Evidence Number Three." Accessed on May 7, 2008. http://www.answersingenesis.org/articles/am/v3/n3/transcontinental-rock-layers.

[123] Ibid.

[124] John Morris "Young Earth – Science" (ppt. presentation, Institute for Creation Science, Santee, California. n.d.).

[125] *Encyclopaedia Britannica Online,* s.v. "Sauk Sequence," accessed November 10, 2012. http://www.britannica.com/EBchecked/topic/525438/Sauk-Sequence.

[126] *Wikipedia,* s.v. "Sauk Sequence," Accessed on November 10, 2012, http://en.wikipedia.org/wiki/Sauk_sequence.

[127] James S. Monroe and Reed Wicander. *The Changing Earth: Exploring Geology and Evolution,* 2nd ed. (Belmont: West Publishing Company, 1997), 533.

[128] Ibid.

[129] *Encyclopaedia Britannica Online,* s.v. "Great Artesian Basin," accessed November 10, 2012, http://wwwbritannica.com/EBchecked/topic/242865/Great-Artesian-Basin.

[130] Tas Walker, "The Great Artesian Basin, Australia," *CEN Tech. Journal,* 10, no. 3 (1996):.382http://creation.com/images/pdfs/tj/j10_3/j10_3_379-390.pdf.

[131] D.V. Ager, *The Nature of the Stratigraphical Record,* (London: Macmillan, 1973), 1–2.

[132] Andrew Snelling, "Transcontinental Rock Layers: Flood Evidence Number Three," Accessed on November, 2012, http://www.answersingenesis.org/articles/am/v3/n3/transcontinental-rock-layers.

[133] J. R. Baumgardner, "John R. Baumgardner: Geophysics."

[134] G. Berthault, "Experiments on lamination of sediments," *Compte Rendus Académie des Sciences Paris* t.303, Série II, no. 17 (1986): 1569-1574; and *CEN Tech. J.* 3 (1988): 25-29. Also, P.Y. Julien, Y. Lan, and G. Berthault, "Experiments on stratification of heterogeneous sand mixtures," *Bulletin of the Geological Society of France* 164, no.5 (1993): 649-660; and *CEN Tech. J.* 8, no. 1(1994): 37-50. See also http://creation.com/sedimentation-experiments-is-extrapolation-appropriate-a-reply.

[135] K. Carpenter, K.F. Hirsch and J.R. Homer eds., *Dinosaur Eggs and Babies,* (London: Cambridge University Press, 1994), 347-365. The discovery is written up in Lockley, M.G., "Dinosaur ontogeny and population structure: interpretations and speculations based on fossil footprints."

[136] Michael Oard, "In the Footsteps of Giants," *Creation* 25, no. 2 (March 2003): 10-12, http://creation.com/in-the-footsteps-of-giants.

[137] Colin Patterson, "Patterson Misquoted A Tale of Two 'Cites'." Accessed on November 10, 2012, http://www.talkorigins.org/faqs/patterson.html.

[138] L. Sunderland, *Darwin's Enigma*, (Arkansas: Master Books, 1998), 101-102. Patterson's letter was written in 1979; Ref. Patterson, personal communication. L. Sutherland, *Darwin's Enigma*, (El Cajon, CA: Master Books, 1988), 88-90.

[139] Gary Bates, "That quote! – about the missing transitional fossils: Embarrassed evolutionists try to 'muddy the waters,'" *Creation* 29, no. 1 (December 2006): 12-15, http://creation.com/that-quoteabout-the-mising-transitional-fossils.

[140] C.R. Darwin, *Origin of Species*, 6th edition, 1872 (London: John Murray, 1902), 413.

[141] S.J. Gould, *Evolution Now: A Century After Darwin*, ed. John Maynard Smith, (New York: Macmillan Publishing Co., 1982), 140.

[142] Full name: *Tiktaalitroseae* – *Tiktaalik* from the Inuit word for burbot, (a large, shallow freshwater fish); *roseae* is a cryptic reference to the anonymous donor who funded the expedition.

[143] Jerry Coyne, *Why Evolution*, 37.

[144] Ibid., 38.

[145] Richard Dawkins, *The Greatest Show on Earth: The Evidence for Evolution*, (Free Press, 2009).

[146] Jonathan Safarti, "Tiktaalik roseae – a fishy 'missing link,'" Accessed on November 10, 2012, http://creation.com/tiktaalik-roseae-a-fishy-missing-link.

[147] Grzegorz Niedźwiedzki, Piotr Szrek, Katarzyna Narkiewicz, MarekNarkiewicz and Per E. Ahlberg, "Tetrapod trackways from the early Middle Devonian period of Poland," *Nature* 463 (January 7, 2010): 43-48. doi:10.1038/nature08623.

[148] Rebecca Conolly and Russell Grigg, "Flood!" *Creation*, 23, no. 1 (December 2000) 26-30, http://creation.com/many-flood-legends is a good example of this.

[149] Michael Oard: *An Ice Age Caused by the Genesis Flood*, (Institute For Creation Research, 1990).

[150] Larry Vardiman, "Jerusalem's Unique Climate," Accessed on November 10, 2012, http://www.icr.org/i/pdf/imp/imp-320.pdf.

[151] *Encyclopaedia Britannica*, 15th ed., s.v. "elephant."

[152] Andrew Snelling, "How did millions of mammoth fossils form?" Accessed on November 10, 2012, http://creation.com/how-did-millions-of-mammoth-fossils-form.

[153] *TJ* 17, no. 2 (2003):78.

[154] *TJ* 17, no. 2 (2003):76-77.

[155] Luigi L. Cavalli-Sforza, *Genes, Peoples and Languages*, (London: Penguin Books, 2001) reviewed by Alexander R. Williams, *TJ* 16, no. 2 (2002): 37-39, http://creation.com/images/pdfs/tj/j16_2/j16_2_37-39.pdf, estimates the number to be 17.

[156] M. Ruhlen, "The origin of the Na-Dene," *Proceedings of the National Academy of Sciences*, 95 (1998): 13994-13996. Quoted in C. Wieland, "Siberian Links for Amerindians," *Creation* 21, no. 3 (1999): 9. This latter possibility is illustrated by the finding of links between the Siberian Ket language and the North American Na Dene language.

[157] K. J. Duursma, "The Tower of Babel account confirmed by linguistics." *Journal of Creation* 16, no. 3 (December 2002): 27-31.

[158] J.C. Gutin, "End of the rainbow," *Discover*, (November 1994):71-75, http://creation.com/images/pdfs/cabook/chapter18.pdf.

[159] Duana Fullwiley, "Race and Genetics: Attempts to Define the Relationship," *Biosocieties*, 2 (2007):221-237. doi:10.1017/S1745855207005625.

[160] P. Cohen, "Redheads Come Out of the Shade," *New Scientist* 147 (1997): 18, http://creation.com/one-blood-chapter-4-one-race. Other substances can in minor ways affect skin shading, such as the colored fibers of the protein elastin and the pigment carotene. However, once again we all share these same compounds, and the principles governing their inheritance are similar to those outlined here. Factors other than pigment in the skin may influence the shade perceived by the observer in subtle ways, such as the thickness of the overlying (clear) skin layers, the density and positioning of the blood capillary networks,

etc. In fact, 'melanin,' which is produced by cells in the body called melanocytes, consists of two pigments, which also account for hair color. Eumelanin is very dark brown, phaeomelanin is more reddish. People tan when sunlight stimulates eumelanin production. Redheads, who are often unable to develop a protective tan, have a high proportion of phaeomelanin. They have probably inherited a defective gene which makes their pigment cells 'unable to respond to normal signals that stimulate eumelanin production.'

[161] Sandford, p.155.

[162] D.R. Humphreys, interview by Carl Weiland, "Creation in the Physics Lab," *Creation* 15, no. 3 (June 1993):20-23, http://creation.com/creation-in-the-physics-lab-creation-magazine-russell-humphreys.

[163] A. Edmond Mathezmd, ed., "James Hutton: The Founder of Modern Geology," *Earth: Inside and Out.* Accessed on November 10, 2012, http://www.amnh.org/education/resources/rfl/web/essaybooks/earth/p_hutton.html.

[164] The inner core is solid and about 1200 km. thick. The outer core is liquid and about 2300 km. thick. See http://scign.jpl.nasa.gov/learn/plate1.htm.

[165] Paul Demorest, "Dynamo Theory and Earth's Magnetic Field," (May 21, 2001), http://setiathome.berkeley.edu/~pauld/etc/210BPaper.pdf. "Using values given by Moffat for the core...we get $t=1.5^4$ years. Since the age of the Earth, and the geological record of the field span a much longer time thanthis, we can take this calculation as evidence of a fluid dynamo in the coreacting to perpetuate the field."

[166] Richard Fitzpatrick, Accessed on November 10, 2012, http://farside.ph.utexas.edu/teaching/plasma/lectures1/node71.html.

[167] A.J. Dessler, "Does Uranus Have a Magnetic Field?" *Nature*, 316, no. 16 (January 1986): 174-175.

[168] Russell Humphreys, interview with *Creation* 15, no. 3 (June 1993): 20-23, http://creation.com/creation-in-the-physics-lab-creation-magazine-russell-humphreys.

[169] D. Russell Humphreys, "Beyond Neptune: Voyager II Supports Creation," retrieved from http://www.icr.org/article/329/ His footnote [8] is A.R. Kerr, "The Neptune system in Voyager's afterglow," *Science*,

245 (29 September 1989): 1450-1451. [9] is D.R. Humphreys, "Good news from Neptune: The Voyager II Magnetic Measurements," *Creation Research Society Quarterly* (1990), in press at the time.

[170] E.N. Parker, E.N. "Magnetic fields in the cosmos," *Scientific American,* 249 (August 1983): 44-54, L.L. Hood, "The enigma of lunar magnetism," *EOS,* 62 (21 April 1981): 161-163. See also D.R. Humphreys, "The creation of planetary magnetic fields," *Creation Research Society Quarterly,* 25 (December 1984): 140-149. Available from Creation Research Society, P.O. Box 14016, Terre Haute, Indiana 47803.

[171] M.T. Bland, A.P. Showman, and G. Tobie, "The production of Ganymede's magnetic field," *Icarus,* 198 (2008): 384-399.

[172] Ganymede, Wayne Spencer, "The Surprisingly Magnetic Moon," *Journal of Creation* 23, no. 1 (April 2009): 8-9.

[173] F. Bagenal, "The emptiest magnetosphere," *Physics World,* (October 1989): 18-19.

[174] D. Russell Humphreys, "The Earth's Magnetic Field Is Young." Accessed on November 10, 2012, http://www.icr.org/article/earths-magnetic-field-young/.

[175] Quadrupole, octopole, etc.

[176] D. Russell Humphreys, "The Earth's Magnetic Field is Still Losing Energy," *CRSQ* 39, no. 1 (June 2002): 1-11, http://www.creationresearch.org/crsq/articles/39/39_1/GeoMag.htm.

[177] David Malcolm, "Helium in the Earth's Atmosphere," *TJ* 8, no.2 (August 1994): 142-147. The sources he cites are: G.J.F. MacDonald, "The escape of helium from the earth's atmosphere," *Reviews of Geophysics and Space Physics* 1 (1963): 305-349; G.J.F. P.J. Brancazio and A.G.W. Cameron, eds., *The Origin and Evolution of Atmospheres and Oceans,* (New York: John Wiley and Sons, 1964), 74-85, 127-128; K.K. Turekian, *Degassing of Argon and Helium from the earth,* (New York: Wiley, 1964), 74; I.W. Axford, "The polar wind and the terrestrial helium budget," *Journal of Geophysical Research* 73 (1968): 6855-6859; H. Craig and W.B. Clarke, "Oceanic ^{3}He: Contribution from cosmogenic tritium," *Earth and Planetary Science Letters,* 10 (1970): 289-296.

[178] The more precise number is $(3.71\pm0.04) \times 10.^{15}$

[179] Larry Vardiman, "The Age of the Earth's Atmosphere Estimated by its Helium Content." Paper presented at the First International Conference on Creationism, Pittsburgh, Pennsylvania, August 4-9, 1986. Published in R.E. Walsh, C.L. Brooks, & R.S. Crowell, eds., *Proceedings of the First International Conference on Creationism,* (Pittsburgh, PA: Creation Science Fellowship, Inc., 1986), 187-194, http://static.icr.org/i/pdf/technical/The-Age-of-Earths-Atmosphere-by-its-Helium-Content.pdf. "The long-age model has for many years assumed no primordial helium in the earth or atmosphere. However, the recent discovery by Clarke, Beg, & Craig (1969) of ^{3}He leaking through the crust has forced the recognition of primordial helium in the mantle. This admission was necessary because no known radioactive decay process in the mantle is known to produce ^{3}He. Now it is recognized that at least a small portion of the ^{4}He is also primordial. The question then arises, if primordial helium can exist in the mantle, why could it not have also existed in the atmosphere when the atmosphere was formed?"

[180] The term is named after: J.H. Jeans, *The Dynamical Theory of Gases,* (London: Cambridge University Press, 1965).

[181] J.C.G. Walker, *Evolution of the Atmosphere* (New York: Macmillan Publishing Co., 1977), 151. Quoted in Malcolm, "Helium."

[182] Malcolm, "Helium," citing MacDonald, G. J. F "The escape of helium," (1964) from the earth's atmosphere. Also quoted in P. J. Brancazio and A. G. W. Cameron, eds., *The Origins and Evolution,"* 127–182.

[183] NASA, "Solar Wind Squeezes some of Earth's Atmosphere into Space," press release, December 8, 1998.

[184] Montana State University Department of Solar Physics, accessed on November 12, 2012, http://solar.physics.montana.edu/press/faq.html.

[185] "The Sunspot Cycle." Accessed on November 12, 2012, http://solarscience.msfc.nasa.gov/SunspotCycle.shtml.

[186] "Yearly Averaged Sunspot Numbers 1610-2010." Accessed on November 12, 2012, http://solarscience.msfc.nasa.gov/images/ssn_yearly.jpg.

[187] K.B. Ramesh, *The Astrophysical Journal Letters*, 712, no. 1 (2010): L77-L80, http://adsabs.harvard.edu/abs/2010ApJ...712L..77R.

[188] Mary H. Schweitzer, Wenxia Zheng, Chris L. Organ, Recep Avci, Zhiyong Suo, Lisa M. Freimark, Valerie S. Lebleu, Michael B. Duncan, Matthew G. Vander Heiden, John M. Neveu, William S. Lane, John S. Cottrell, John R. Horner, Lewis C. Cantley, Raghu Kalluri, and John M. Asara, "Biomolecular Characterization and Protein Sequences of the Campanian Hadrosaur B. Canadensis," *Science* 324, no.5927 (May 1, 2009): 626-631.doi: 10.1126/science.1165069.

[189] M. Schweitzer and I. Staedter, "The Real Jurassic Park," *Earth*, (June 1997): 55-57.

[190] M.H. Schweitzer, Z. Suo, R. Avci, J.M. Asara, A.M. Allen, F.T. Arce, and J.R. Homer, "Analyses of soft tissue from Tyrannosaurus rex suggest the presence of protein," *Science*, 316, no. 5822 (2007): 277-280; and J.M. Asara, M.H. Schweitzer, L.M. Freimark, M. Phillips, and L.C. Cantley, "Protein sequences from mastodon and Tyrannosaurus rex revealed by mass spectrometry," *Science*, 316, no. 5822 (2007): 280-285.

[191] Clade - a group of creatures sharing similar features believed to be descended from a common ancestor.

[192] Shaun Doyle, Squishosaur scepticism squashed. Tests confirm proteins found in T. rex bones, Accessed on November 12, 2012, http://creation.com/squishosaur-scepticism-squashed.

[193] J. Bada, J. et al., 'Preservation of key biomolecules in the fossil record: current knowledge and future challenges.' *Philosophical Transactions of the Royal Society B: Biological Sciences*, 354, no. 1379 (1999): 77-87 See as well C. Nielsen-Marsh, "Biomolecules in Fossil Remains: A Multidisciplinary Approach to Endurance," *The Biochemist*, (June 2002): 12–14.

[194] T. Kaye et al., "Dinosaurian Soft Tissues Interpreted as Bacterial Biofilms," *PloS One,* (July 30, 2008), plosone.org.

[195] Brian Thomas, M.S. "Dinosaur Soft Tissue: Biofilm or Blood Vessels?" Accessed on November 12, 2012, http://www.icr.org/article/dinosaur-soft-tissue-biofilm-or-blood-vessels/. His reference [6] is T. Peake, "Small Foot, Big Impression." North Carolina State University

online feature, July 24, 2007. [7] is J. Roach, "Dinosaur Slime Sparks Debate Over Soft Tissue Finds." *National Geographic News*, posted online July 30, 2008, accessed August 22, 2008.

[196] Helen Fields, "Dinosaur Shocker," *Smithsonian magazine*, (May 2006). http://www.smithsonianmag.com/science-nature/10021606.html. The name B. rex is in honour of Bob Harmon of the Museum of the Rockies who first discovered it. It turns out that Bob rex was actually a pregnant female.

[197] Philip Bell, "Bishop Bell's Brass Behemoths," *Creation* 25, no. 4 (September 2003): 40-44, http://creation.com/bishop-bells-brass-behemoths.

[198] Phil Senter and S. J. Cole, "Dinosaur petroglyphs at Kachina Bridge site, Natural Bridges National Monument, southeastern Utah: not dinosaurs after all," *Palaeontologia Electronica* 14, no. 1 (2011): 1–5.

[199] Ishmael Abrahams, "Feedback: Kachina Bridge Dinosaur Petroglyph: Still Good Evidence." Accessed on November 12, 2012. http://www.answersingenesis.org/articles/2011/03/18/feedback-senter-and-cole.

[200] The formula is $^1n + {}^{14}N \rightarrow {}^{14}C + {}^1p$.

[201] Jonathan Sarfati, "Diamonds: a creationist's best friend. Radiocarbon in diamonds; enemy of billions of years," *Creation* 28, no.4 (September 2006): 26-27, http://creation.com/diamonds-a-creationists-best-friend "The earth's mass is 6×10^{27} g; equivalent to 4.3×10^{26} moles of ^{14}C. Each mole contains Avogadro's number ($N_A = 6.022 \times 10^{23}$) of atoms. It takes only 167 halvings to get down to a single atom ($\log_2(4.3 \times 10^{26}$ mol $\times 6.022 \times 10^{23}$ mol$^{-1}) = \log_{10}(2.58 \times 10^{50}) / \log_{10} 2$), and 167 half-lives is well under a million years."

[202] R.L. Whitelaw, "Time, life and history in the light of 15,000 radiocarbon dates," *Creation Research Society Quarterly* 7, no. 1 (1970): 56-71, http://creationresearch.org/crsq-abstracts/sum7_1.html.

[203] J.R. Baumgardner, "^{14}C Evidence for a Recent Global Flood and a Young Earth," *Radioisotopes and the Age of the Earth*, (El Cajon, CA: Institute for Creation Research, 2005), 588, 589.

[204] Ibid., 587-588.

[205] Ibid., Table 1, 596-597.
[206] Diamond Wholesale Corporation. Accessed on November 12, 2012, http:/diamondwholesalecorporation.com/diamond-knowledge-2/scientific-facts/
[207] Tetsuo Irifune, Ayako Kurio, Shizue Sakamoto, Toru Inoue & Hitoshi Sumiya, "*Materials: Ultrahard polycrystalline diamond from graphite,*" Nature 421, nos. 599-600 (February 6, 2003). doi:10.1038/421599b.
[208] J.R. Baumgardner, *^{14}C Evidence,* 611.
[209] Jonathan Sarfati, "Diamonds."
[210] Ibid.
[211] Laboratories and analysts who performed the measurements were XRAL Laboratories of S.G.S Canada, Don Mills, Ont. Jan. 1997 and Feb. 2002; Dr. R. Reesman, Geochron Laboratories, Cambridge, Mass.; Assoc. Prof. G. L. Farmer, University of Colorado; Dr. Y. Kapusta, Activation Laboratories, Ancaster Ont. These labs measured the samples mentioned in this document and/or others found in Austin's chapter in R.AT.E. (See below). The analyses were limited to accurate measurements of the respective isotopes and did not proffer age estimates.
[212] Andrew Snelling, "Radioisotope dating of rocks in the Grand Canyon," http://creation.com/radioisotope-dating-of-rocks-in-the-grand-canyon originally published in *Creation* 27, no. 3 (June 2005): 44-49.
[213] Ibid. "An isochron is a graphical plot of the isotopic compositions of the samples. It allows an isochron age to be calculated from a straight line plotted through the graph of the results. The Isoplot computer program, developed by Dr. Ken Ludwig at the University Of California Berkeley Geochronology Center, was used. See: Ludwig, K.R., *Isoplot/ Ex (Version 2.49): The Geochronological Toolkit for Excel,* University of California Berkeley, Berkeley Geochronology Center, Special Publication No. 1a, 2001. The method effectively requires multiple assumptions, namely that the initial isotopic ratio of each sample was the same as the ratio of every other sample in the group."
[214] Ibid.

215 The remaining 8 samples were outside the line of best fit and thus not included. Similarly for the Sm-Nd and Pb-Pb methods.

216 R.A.T.E., 325.

217 Kenya National Museum East [lake] Rudolf [now Turkana] acquisition number 1470.

218 F.J. Fitch and J.A. Miller, "Radioisotopic Age Determinations of Lake Rudolf Artifact Site," *Nature* 226 (April 18, 1970): 226.

219 Ibid., 228.

220 Marvin Lubenow, "The Pigs Took it All." First published in *Creation* 17, no. 3 (June 1995): 36-38, http://creation.com/the-pigs-took-it-all. Note [4] is Vincent J. Maglio, "*Vertebrate Faunas and Chronology of Hominid-bearing Sediments East of Lake Rudolf, Kenya,*" *Nature* 239 (October 13, 1972): 379–85. Note [5] is A. Brock and G. Isaac, "Paleomagnetic stratigraphy and chronology of hominid-bearing sediments east of Lake Rudolf, Kenya," *Nature* 247 (February 8, 1974): 344–8. Note [6] is Ibid 347.

221 Ibid.

222 Ibid.

223 Andrew Snelling, "Radiohalos: Startling evidence of catastrophic geologic processes on a young earth," first published *Creation* 28, no.2 (March 2006): 46-50, http://creation.com/radiohalosstartling-evidence-of-catastrophic-geologic-processes-on-a-young-earth. "The last three rings of a uranium halo are produced by an element called polonium. Marie Curie (with her husband, Pierre) discovered it in 1898 and named it after her homeland, Poland. One of the important features of radioactive polonium is that it decays rapidly and thus is rarely found in nature. However, it is continually generated when uranium decays, and so radioactive polonium is always associated with uranium."

224 Ibid.

225 R.A.T.E. Vol. 2, 101- 102.

226 D. Russell Humphreys, *Accelerated Nuclear Decay: A Viable Hypothesis?* R.A.T.E. Vol.1, 371.

227 Jonathan Sarfati, "The moon: the light that rules the night," http://creation.com/the-moon-the-light-that-rules-the-night. "For the technical reader: since tidal forces are inversely proportional to the cube

of the distance, the recession rate (dR/dt) is inversely proportional to the *sixth power* of the distance. So dR/dt = k/R^6, where k is a constant = (present speed: 0.04 m/year) x (present distance: 384,400,000 m)^6 = 1.29x10^{50} m^7/year. Integrating this differential equation gives the time to move from R_i to R_f as t = $^1/_{7k}$(R_f^7 — R_i^7). For R_f = the present distance and R_i = the Roche Limit, t = 1.37 x 10^9 years. There is no significant difference if R_i = 0, i.e. the earth and moon touching, because of the high recession rate (caused by enormous tides) if the moon is close."

[228] Apollo 14 Mission, Accessed on November 12, 2012, http://ww.lpi.usra.edu/lunar/missions/apollo/apollo_14/experiments/lrr/.

[229] E.g., K. Hansen, "Secular effects of oceanic tidal dissipation on the moon's orbit and the earth's rotation," *Reviews of Geophysics and Space Physics* 20 (1982): 457-480; J. Piper, *Movements of the continental crust and lithosphere-asthenosphere systems in Precambrian times*, in P. Brosche, and J. Sundermann, eds., *Tidal Friction and the Earth's Rotation II*, (Berlin: Springer-Verlag, 1982): 253-321. Quoted by Jonathan Henry, "The Moon's Recession and Age," *Journal of Creation* 20, no. 2 (August 2006): 65-70.

[230] Jonathan Henry," The Moon's recession and Age." Accessed on November 14, 2012, http://creation.com/the-moons-recession-and-age/.

[231] Jack J. Lissauer, "It's Not Easy to Make the Moon," *Nature* 389, (September 25, 1997): doi:10.1038/38596.

[232] Carl Sagan and George Mullen, "Earth and Mars: Evolution of Atmospheres and Surface Temperatures," *Science* 177, no. 4043 (July 7, 1972): 52-56.doi: 10.1126/science.177.40.

[233] Eric Wolf and Brian Toon, "Early Faint-Sun Paradox Explained," on Space Fellowship, http://spacefellowship.com/new/art20666/early-faint-sun-paradox-explained.html. This is a paper by Wolf and CU-Boulder Professor Brian Toon of the atmospheric and oceanic sciences department. NASA's Planetary Atmosphere Program funded the study.

[234] Minik T. Rosing, Dennis K. Bird, Norman, H. Sleep & Christian J. Bjerrum, "No climate paradox under the faint early Sun," *Nature* 464 (April 1, 2010): 744-747. doi:10.1038/nature08955.

²³⁵ The actual English translation of the Latin reads: *one should not increase, beyond what is necessary, the number of entities required to explain anything.* Though not actually found in Occam's writings in this particular wording its equivalent "*It is futile to do with more things that which can be done with fewer*" is found in his *Summa Totius Logicae*, i. 12 See http://pespmc1.vub.ac.be/occamraz.html and http://en.wikipedia.org/wiki/Occam's_razor.

²³⁶ I am basing this on a paper by Ronald G. Samec, PhD, "The Age of the Jovian Planets," *CEN Technical Journal* (now *Journal of Creation*) 14, no. 1 (2000). As of the date of publication he had 144 professional publications abstracted on the SAO/NASA Astrophysical Data System (ADS).

²³⁷ R. Ouyed, W.R. Fundamenski, G.R. Cripps, and P.G. Sutherland, "D-D fusion in the interior of Jupiter?" *Astrophysical J.* 501(1998): 367–374. Quoted in Samec, "The Age."

²³⁸ Cornell University: Astronomy. Accessed on November 14, 2012, http://astro.cornell.edu/academics/courses/astro2201/vt.htm.

²³⁹ M. Zewlik, S.A. Gregory and E.v.P. Smith, *Introductory Astronomy and Astrophysics*, 3ʳᵈ ed., (Philadelphia: Saunders, Harcourt Brace Jovanovich College Publishers, 1992), 299. Quoted in Samec, "The Age."

²⁴⁰ R. Ouyed, W.R. Fundamenski, G.R. Cripps, and P.G. Sutherland, "D-D fusion in the interior of Jupiter?" *Astrophysical J.* 501 (1998): 367-374. Quoted in Samec, "The Age."

²⁴¹ T. Guillot, G. Chabrier, D. Gautier, and P. Morel, "Effect of radiative transport on the evolution of Jupiter and Saturn," *Astrophysical J.* 450, no. 1 (1995): 463.

²⁴² W.J. Nellis, M. Ross, and N.C. Holmes, "Temperature measurements of shock-compressed liquid hydrogen: implications for the interior of Jupiter," *Science* 269, no. 5228 (1995): 1249-1252. See Ouyed et al as well. Quoted in Samec, "The Age."

²⁴³ Ouyed, "D-D fusion."

²⁴⁴ Ordinary hydrogen lacks the neutron.

²⁴⁵ *Wikipedia*, s.v. "Fusion power," last modified November 6, 2012, http://en.wikipedia.org/wiki/Fusion_power. The temperature required

is 15keV which is approximately 171 million Kelvin. () Samec, "The Age," has a figure 3 orders of magnitude lower and notes: "To convert temperature from eV (electron volts) to kelvins in this situation requires a number of physical assumptions that are not absolutely certain. Consequently astronomers usually quote temperatures in eV in these cases. The following equation was used here to make the conversion: E = 3/2 kT, where E is energy in joules (J), k is Boltzmann's constant = 1.381×10^{-23} J/K, T is temperature in K, and 1 eV = 1.602×10^{-19} J."

[246] Samec, "The Age."

[247] D. Russell Humphreys, "Evidence For a Young World," Accessed on November 12, 2012, http://creation.com/evidence-for-a-young-world. No.[1] is H. Scheffler and H. Elsasser, *Physics of the Galaxy and Interstellar Matter*, (Berlin: Springer-Verlag, 1987), 352-353, 401-413. No.[2] is D. Zaritsky et al., *Nature* (July 22, 1993). *Sky & Telescope*, (December 1993): 10.

[248] Current World Population: Current World Population and World Population Growth Since the Year One. Accessed on November 12, 2012, http://geography.about.com/od/obtainpopulationdata/a/worldpopulation.htm. Also for ethno linguistic estimates see Patrick Johnstone, *Operation World*, (Grand Rapids: Zondervan Publishing House, 1993), 20-22. Though obviously dated, his ethno-linguistic estimates are probably a reasonable approximation for the current context.

[249] Henry M. Morris, Ph.D., *The Biblical Basis for Modern Science*, (Grand Rapids, MI: Baker Book House, 1984), 417, 418.

[250] Philip Kitcher, *Abusing Science: The Case Against Creationism*, (Cambridge, MA: The MIT Press, 1983), 163.

[251] D. Russell Humphreys, "Evidence For A Young World," Accessed on November 12, 2012, n.d.http://creation.com/evidence-for-a-young-world.

[252] Morris, *Biblical Basis*, 420.

[253] Steven Robinson, "From the Flood to the Exodus: Egypt's Earliest Settlers" *Creation ex Nihilo Technical Journal,*(now *Journal of Creation*), 9, part 1 (1995): 45-68, in particular, 64, 65.

[254] Jason Lisle, "Light travel time a problem for the big bang," *Creation* 25, no. 4 (September 2003): 48-49. No.[1] refers to P. Coles and F. Lucchin, *Cosmology: The Origin and Evolution of Cosmic Structure*, (Chichester: John Wiley & Sons Ltd., 1996), 91. No.[2] is 2.728 K (-270.422°C). No.[3] is J.A. Peacock, *Cosmological Physics*, (Cambridge University Press, 1999), 288. No.[4] his comment: "However, the existence of CMB was actually deduced before big bang cosmology from the spectra of certain molecules in outer space. .

[255] Ibid.

[256] J. Trefil, *The Dark Side of the Universe* (New York: Macmillan Publishing Company, 1988), 3 and 55. Quoted by Jonathan Sarfati, Accessed on November 12, 2012, http://creation.com/refuting-evolution-chapter-7-astronomy. Excerpted from his book, *Refuting Evolution*, (Brisbane, Australia: Answers in Genesis, 1999).

[257] Stephen Hawking, *The Illustrated: A Brief History of Time and Universe in a Nutshell*, (Location Published: Bantam, 2007), 156.

[258] Werner Gitt, "What About the Big Bang?" Accessed on November 14, 2012, http://creation.com/what-about-the-big-bang No.[1] is Marcus Chown, "Let there be light," *New Scientist*, 157, no. 2120 (February 7, 1998): 26-30.

[259] D. Russell Humphreys, *Starlight and Time - Solving the Puzzle of Distant Starlight in a Young Universe*, (Colorado Springs, CO: Master Books, 1995), 67-68.

[260] J. Hartnett, "Does the Bible really describe expansion of the universe?" *Journal of Creation* 25, no. 2 (2011): 125-127. Also, Charles V. Taylor, "Waters Above or Waters Beyond," *CEN Tech. J.* 10, no.2 (1996): 211-213, http://creation.com/images/pdfs/tj/j10_2/j10_2_211-213.pdf.

[261] Cited from: Walter Brown, Jr., *In the Beginning: Compelling Evidence for Creation and the Flood*, Sixth Ed., (Phoenix, AZ: Center for Scientific Creation, 1995),158-162, which also has an excellent overview of this position.

[262] João Magueijo, *Faster Than the Speed of Light: The Story of a Scientific Speculation* (London, William Heinemann, 2003).Reviewed by Andrew Sibley, http://creation.com/images/pdfs/tj/j20_1/j20_1_16-18.pdf.

[263] C is the symbol for the speed of light. From the Latin *celeris* 'swift' or 'fast.'

[264] See Carl Wieland's comments on Paul Davies proposals re VSL in http://creation.com/images/pdfs/tj/j20_1/j20_1_16-18.pdf.

[265] R.M. Hutchins, R. M., *Great Books of the Western World*, 16. *Encyclopaedia Britannica*, s. v. "Ptolemy/Copernicus/Kepler."

[266] John Hartnett, *Starlight, Time and the New Physics* first ed. (Australia: Creation Book Publishers, LLC, 2007), 108, 109.

[267] J. Lisle, "Anisotropic Synchrony Convention – A Solution to the Distant Starlight Problem," *Answers Research Journal* 3 (2010): 191-207, www.answersingenesis.org/articles/arj/v3/n1/anisotropic-synchrony-convention. Lisle quotes, A. Einstein, *Relativity: The special and general Theory*, trans. R.W. Lawson, (New York: Crown Publishers Inc., 1961).

[268] Ibid.

[269] D. Russell Humphreys, "New Time Dilation Helps Creation Cosmology," *Journal of Creation* 22, no. 3 (2008): 84-92, http://creation.com/images/pdfs/tj/j22_3/j22_3_84-92.pdf.

[270] John Hartnett, "Does observational evidence indicate the universe is expanding?-part 1: the case for time dilation. And part 2: the case against expansion," *Journal of Creation* 25, no. 3 (2011): 109-120. For Humphreys, see his "New Vistas of Space-Time," *CEN Tech. J.*, 12, no 2 (1998), http://creation.com/images/pdfs/tj/j12_2/j12_2_195-212.pdf.

About the Author

FRANCIS HUMPHREY HOLDS A B.A. (BISHOP'S UNIVERSITY), A DIP.ED. (McGill University), a M.Div. (Canadian Theological College – now Ambrose University), a Th.M. (Trinity Evangelical Divinity School) and a Ph.D. (McGill University). He is a former lecturer in Old Testament Studies in the Faculté de Théologie Évangélique de Montréal, Acadia University. He was also Pastor of The Peoples Church of Montreal, an evangelical, multi-ethnic congregation in downtown Montreal, until his illness forced him to step down. His thesis "Sensory language and the divine-human relationship in the TENAK" (McGill, 1995) involves a combination of phenomenological and medical analyses of the human exteroceptive sensorium and its implications for the study of the Hebrew Scriptures.

He is married and the father of three adult children. In the summer of 2005 he was diagnosed as having A.L.S. and is grateful to God for the saving and sustaining grace he has experienced through Jesus Christ.

www.ingramcontent.com/pod-product-compliance
Lightning Source LLC
Chambersburg PA
CBHW070146100426
42743CB00013B/2828